DONNA FRAWLEY

100 Ways
to Make
a Difference

Creating Ripples of Love
FOR A LASTING LEGACY

Fiesta

PUBLISHING

Author: Donna Frawley
Editor: Peggy Henrikson, Heart and Soul Editing
Interior Design: Jonathan Lewis, Jonlin Creative
Cover Design: Jonathan Lewis, Jonlin Creative
Cover Photographs: Leaf – iStock.com/BlackJack3D   Background – iStock.com/art Photo
Other Photographs: Donna Frawley or as designated

ISBN: 979-8-9857477-5-1 (Paperback)
         979-8-9857477-6-8 (eBook)

Library of Congress Number: 2022909030

First printing edition 2022

Printed in the United States of America

10 9 8 7 6 5 4 3 2 1

Fiesta Publishing
PO Box 44984
Phoenix, AZ 85064

www.fiestapublishing.com

DEDICATION

I dedicate this book to Jesus,
who tossed the rock that made ripples
to inspire us all to
make a difference.

Continue to make a difference
and make the world a
better place for all.

Wonna Frawley

July 2023

ACKNOWLEDGMENTS

WRITING THIS BOOK has been an interesting journey, with many people encouraging me along the way.

Thank you to the people whose quotes I included. They inspired me, and I hope they will inspire you, my readers.

I also would like to thank my family for always being there to lift me up. I included some stories from my husband Nile, my three daughters Sabrina, Samantha, and Veronica, and their children.

My friend Irene, who is more like a sister, is always my biggest cheerleader. Irene, your encouragement has meant the world to me.

Marcia, you inspired me to do this in the first place when you told our garden club that I made a difference in your life. I was very humbled and inspired to share that with others.

I'm grateful to all my garden club members. You allowed me to speak at our district meeting on "Make a Difference in Your Garden and Beyond" without knowing what I was going to say.

Thank you also to my sisters Sandy, Karen, and Penny for your contributions to the story and to both Penny and her husband George for reading my manuscript and sharing your ideas and encouragement.

Thank you to my pastors, Gerald Ferguson and Danielle Shealy, who asked if I would let them print out my posts, and thank you to those who read them.

Thank you to Peggy Henrikson, my initial editor, for being so meticulous with all the words on the page.

With much gratitude for Julie Castro, my publisher at Fiesta Publishing, for taking a chance on me.

Immense gratitude to You, Lord, for helping me put words on

the page, find Bible verses that went with each day, giving me Peggy and Julie in such miraculous ways, and for loving me.

CONTENTS

PREFACE

I BEGAN THINKING about putting together this book in 2019. I had written a historical fiction novel, and my protagonist made a difference in every person in the story. This prompted me to begin my work on how people can make a difference.

In the process, I learned a lot about myself. I realized I was already doing some things that could possibly make a difference and I needed to work on other ways. If I needed to work on this, maybe others did, too. I immediately came up with 35 ideas then built from there. Along the way, I got more ideas from research, Bible lessons, Sunday sermons, TV commercials, and so on. I seemed to find ideas everywhere I looked.

I saw a TEDx talk where Michelle Poler faced her fears and called it "100 Days Without Fear." That made me wonder what kind of an impact we could have if we could make a difference each day for 100 days.

So, I took my 100 ways to make a difference and began posting them on my Donna Frawley Author Facebook page, where I had a photo for each day as well. Then I added messages to my Instagram account and sent them out five days at a time to my newsletter subscribers.

My pastors approached me and wanted to count back 100 days from December 31, 2020 (the first year of the pandemic) and give people 100 days to finish the year on a positive note. I added Bible verses to back up what I was saying, and our congregation began on September 22 with Day 1.

At some point, I was posting on four different media sites with four different schedules. Keeping track of where I was on each posting was a challenge. Finally, I took those postings, embellished them, added quotes and prayers to each day, and came up with this book. I hope you find it valuable and make a difference in many lives!

"Never underestimate the valuable and important difference you make in every life you touch, for the impact you make today has a powerful rippling effect on every tomorrow."
~ LEON BROWN

Photo from an article by Penny L. Howe:
"The Ripple Effect – How to Succeed in Life!"[1]

INTRODUCTION

OUR WORLD IS full of challenges. Every day on the news we hear more and more of what is wrong in the world. What can we do about it? Nothing? I say, in our own way, we all can make a difference by serving others as the Bible directs us.

> Mark 10:45 ~ "For the Son of Man came
> not to be served but to serve . . ."[2]

Picture a still pond with not a ripple in sight. Then suddenly someone throws a stone, making a splash that produces ripples. Those ripples represent an awakening in us by the Lord's call to action generated by the stone. The ripples are deep and close together in the center. As they radiate outward, they get farther apart and less deep, but ripples are still moving out toward the shore. With the Lord's help at the center, we can be inspired to accept the call and ride the generated ripples outward, touching others' lives in the world. Our ripples may intersect the ripples of others, which only increases the impact of what we can accomplish together. This collaboration never takes away from who we are or what we're contributing; it only adds to our influence.

> "I alone cannot change the world, but I can cast a stone across
> the waters to create many ripples."
> MOTHER TERESA, 1910-1997

Whether you're a Traditionalist (born between 1900 and 1945), a Baby Boomer (1946-1964), a Generation Xer (1965-1980), a

Millennial (1981-2000), or a Generation Zer (2001-), your group is different from the others. However, all groups have a common thread. We all strive to understand one another and work together to make our planet a better place for us and the next generation so we all can lead happy lives. To do this, we need to feel empowered to be a positive influence, not only on people close to us but people in our communities and around the world.

The younger generations may be asking themselves, "What's the meaning of my life? Why am I here? How can I make a difference in the world?" They have a need to change the focus of youth, which is often naturally on dependence, self-centeredness, and entitlement, to a more expanded way of thinking that considers the importance of family and others. They begin to focus on making a difference—not just in their own small sphere of influence but in society as a whole. Some look to work for businesses that don't just concentrate on making a profit but rather on improving the greater world.

The older generations may be wondering if they have made a difference, now that they're closer to the end of their lives than the beginning. Their focus often shifts to giving back to society and helping reduce someone else's hardships. Thus, they become an example to the youth and those around them while leaving a legacy of making a difference to their family and friends.

Whatever your age, if you're asking yourself, *How can I make a difference in the world?* I hope you'll find this book helpful, at least as a start. *Thank you* for wanting to make the world a better place!

The Structure of *100 Ways to Make a Difference*

In thinking about the structure of the book, I thought about my own life. I pictured myself at the center, with God as my rock, initiating the ripples within me. I realized that to be most effective, I needed to make a difference in *myself first* before I progressed outward to make a difference in others' lives.

To help you as you move outward, I created six categories, or levels, in which you can make a difference in . . .

1. yourself,
2. your family,
3. your friends and neighbors,
4. your community,
5. your country, and
6. your world.

Please note: Just because a suggestion is listed under one of the categories (Yourself, Your Family, Your Friends, etc.) doesn't mean it wouldn't fit in another category. Use the suggestions for whatever you want and however you feel guided to use them. They will still make a difference.

After my intense research began, it seemed everything I read or heard pertained to making a difference. It was amazing. I collected 100 items so I'd have one item a day for 100 days. I dispersed my 100 ideas throughout the six categories, knowing many were interchangeable between the categories. I then found quotes that helped drive home each point and Bible verses to meditate on that pertained to the daily topic. I also added a short prayer for each day.

We've all heard of famous people taking on big projects that cost a lot of money. For instance, the Bill & Melinda Gates Foundation spends millions on fighting poverty, disease, and inequity in impoverished nations around the world. The William and Flora Hewlett Foundation also spends millions, targeted to education and agricultural markets for farmers in developing countries. However, as worthwhile as those projects are, not all of us have the funds to do likewise. The ideas to make a difference I present here aren't big projects, and they cost very little, if anything. That doesn't lessen their value or minimize our efforts. We can be just as passionate with our "ripple projects" as those people with their "big splash projects," and we can make a valuable difference in our own way.

Consider Matthew 25:14-30. Jesus tells us about three slaves—one who received five talents (a large amount of money), one who received two talents, and a third who received one talent. The first two used their given talents and increased them, but the third one buried it and gained nothing more. From this story, we learn that none of us have the same talents as another, but we can use what we do have to the glory of God by not hiding our talents and doing good in the world. For example, not all of us can sew, so when the pandemic hit, if everyone were asked to sew masks, it would not have been a good use of everyone's talents. That said, each of us could do something, even if it wasn't sewing masks.

This book suggests you do one thing a day for 100 days to make a difference. If you feel you can't do some of the ideas presented, change them to fit you, come up with your own ideas, or check out the Additional Ideas in the back of the book. What makes a difference is that you're doing *something!* All of us are blessed with God-given talents that can be multiplied if we share those talents with someone else.

> "In a world full of neighbors, someone could use the blessing you
> have to share, whether it be money, friendship, your gifts, or
> skills, or simply your time. Invest wisely."[3]
> ~ Reverend James Smith

It's our duty and can be a joy to shepherd others so they live life abundantly, and by being kind, we share with others the example Jesus demonstrated.

For the next 100 days, this book will offer you ideas of ways you can make a difference. Each chapter will share *why* you should make a difference in that category of yourself, your family, your friends/neighborhood, your community, your country, and your world.

Picture yourself in the center of the pond riding the ripples that God initiated. The ripples begin with God working in you so you can bless others as you move outward. Start making a difference in yourself, and then you can go beyond and make a difference in the lives of others.

You're invited to start your 100-day journey with this wisdom from Holy Father Pope Francis:

Rivers do not drink their own water;
trees do not eat their own fruit;
the sun does not shine on itself and
flowers do not spread their fragrance for themselves.
Living for others is a rule of nature.
We are born to help each other.
No matter how difficult it is.
Life is good when you are happy
but much better when others are happy because of you.
Let us remember that pain is a sign that we are alive,
problems are a sign that we are strong and
prayer is a sign that we are not alone.
If we can acknowledge these truths and
condition our hearts and minds, our lives will be more meaningful,
different
and
worthwhile.[4]

CHAPTER 1

MAKE A DIFFERENCE IN YOURSELF

WHEN YOU'RE READY, jump right in. The first 21 days will involve things you can do to make a difference in yourself.

Why Make a Difference in Yourself?
Six good reasons are to:

1. find the good within yourself so you can shine your light in your own way;
2. give yourself a purpose;
3. make others feel better about themselves, knowing you care about yourself;
4. make yourself healthier physically, mentally, spiritually, and emotionally;
5. encourage yourself to do more because one thing leads to another;
6. make the world a better place to live—one small step at a time—starting with you.

PLANT A TREE.

IF YOU DON'T have a spot for a tree outside, what about an inside tree such as a Norfolk Island Pine, Ficus Benjamina, or Meyer Lemon? Or root an avocado pit and start growing your own tree.

Planting a tree can make you feel good because of a tree's many benefits:

1. A tree gives you something outside of yourself to care for, reducing stress and anxiety.
2. A tree takes in carbon dioxide and gives off oxygen to help the environment.
3. A tree planted outdoors creates a place to house birds and other wildlife.
4. Trees prevent soil erosion and rainwater runoff.
5. Trees produce shade in the summer, keeping your house cooler.
6. Trees help break the wind in the winter, keeping your house warmer.
7. Trees produce a legacy for future generations.
8. A fruit tree helps feed people.
9. Trees add beauty.

My husband Nile and I have a large city lot, about three-quarters of an acre, where we've planted 35 fruit trees. They give us shade, beautiful blooms in the spring, and bushels of fruit during the growing season. Any extra fruit gets boxed up and given to Hidden Harvest, which is shared with soup kitchens and food pantries, where we can make a difference.

One of the 35 fruit trees on our lot

"The one who plants trees, knowing that he will never sit in their shade, has at least started to understand the meaning of life."
~ RABINDRANATH TAGORE

Plant a Tree
by Lucy Larcom (1824-1893)

He who plants a tree
Plants a hope. . . .
Plants a joy; . . .
He plants peace. . . .
He plants youth; . . .

He plants love, . . .
Plant! Life does the rest!
Heaven and earth help him who plants a tree,
And his work its own reward shall be.[5]

Genesis 1:12 ~ "The earth brought forth vegetation: plants yielding seed of every kind, and trees of every kind bearing fruit with the seed in it. And God saw that it was good."

Matthew 13:31-32 ~ "He put before them another parable: "The kingdom of heaven is like a mustard seed that someone took and sowed in his field; it is the smallest of all the seeds, but when it has grown, it is the greatest of shrubs and becomes a tree, so that the birds of the air come and make nests in its branches."

Prayer
Dear Heavenly Father,
As the tree reaches for heaven as it grows, help me grow in faith as I reach for Your guidance. Amen.

DAY 2: YOURSELF

TELL SOMEONE YOU'RE SORRY.

MANY REASONS MAY arise for needing to tell someone you're sorry: You may have hurt their feelings, betrayed a confidence, or caused them to suffer in some way. You may be sorry something bad happened to them. You apologize by admitting your fault, if you were involved in some way. This can reduce or eliminate their suffering. This action makes both of you feel better, either sustaining a lasting relationship or mending a broken one. Being genuinely sorry touches hearts and makes a difference.

> "Mistakes are always forgivable if one has
> the courage to admit them."
> ~ BRUCE LEE (1940-1973)

"No act of kindness no matter how small is ever wasted."
~AESOP (620-564 BCE)

Psalm 38:18 ~ "I confess my iniquity; I am sorry for my sin."

James 5:16 ~ "Therefore, confess your sins to one another, and pray for one another, so that you may be healed. The prayer of the righteous is powerful and effective."

Prayer
Good and gracious God,
Open the hearts of the people to which I say "I am sorry" so they will accept my apology and build or mend our relationship. Amen.

DAY 3: YOURSELF

TELL SOMEONE YOU FORGIVE THEM.

FORGIVING SOMEONE HELPS both you and them. They feel renewed with the knowledge you don't hold something against them, and you don't have to spend any more time thinking about how they wronged you.

The someone you forgive could be yourself. We are very hard on ourselves, some more than others. Forgiving ourselves aids in our well-being and sparks a better positive attitude, which improves our relationships with others.

So, whether you forgive yourself or someone else, the overall benefit is a fresh start all around and it will definitely make a difference.

"It's one of the greatest gifts you can give yourself, to forgive."
~ MAYA ANGELOU (1928-2014)

"Forgiveness is a strange thing. It can sometimes be easier to forgive our enemies than our friends. It can be hardest of all to forgive people we love. Like all of life's important coping skills,

the ability to forgive and the capacity to let go of resentments most likely take root very early in our lives."
~ Mr. (Fred) Rogers (1928-2003)

Genesis 50:17 ~ (For the whole story, read Genesis 37-50.) Years after his brothers sold him, Joseph forgave them. They came to him and told him their father had commanded them before he died: "Say to Joseph: 'I beg you, forgive the crime of your brothers and the wrong they did in harming you.' Now therefore please forgive the crime of the servants of the God of your father. Joseph wept when they spoke to him."

Matthew 6:15 ~ ". . . but if you do not forgive others, neither will your Father forgive your trespasses."

Prayer
Dear God,
I ask you to forgive me and help me forgive myself for the things I have done wrong and the things I should have done. You want me to have a life of joy and peace. I can only attain that with forgiveness. Thank you, Lord. Amen.

DAY 4: YOURSELF

MAKE SOMEONE LAUGH.

You never know what has affected someone's mood for the day. By making someone laugh, it can change their whole outlook for the rest of the day. Tell a joke or a funny story, or share a funny cartoon with them. If you are the one who is down, watch a video of Stan Laurel laughing on YouTube. It could really make a difference! I once heard a television announcer say after watching Stan Laurel, "If you aren't laughing after that, I'm sorry to tell you, you may be dead."

Have a laugh at this quote by Dave Barry:

"My therapist told me the way to achieve true inner peace is to finish what I start. So far, I've finished two bags of M&M's and a chocolate cake. I feel better already."

"If I were given the opportunity to present a gift to the next generation, it would be the ability for each individual to learn to laugh at himself."
~ CHARLES M. SCHULZ (1922-2000), WHO CREATED THE MUCH-BELOVED COMIC STRIP *PEANUTS*

"If one has no sense of humor, one is in trouble."
~ BETTY WHITE (1922-2021)

Psalm 126:2 ~ "Then our mouth was filled with laughter, and our tongue with shouts of joy; then it was said among the nations, 'The Lord has done great things for them.'"

John 15:11 ~ "I have said these things to you so that my joy may be in you, and that your joy may be complete."

Prayer
Hello, Jesus.
Thank You for the gift of laughter. Being able to laugh at myself for the funny things I do is a blessing. I believe You have a wonderful sense of humor, as seen in so many parts of Creation. Help me lighten up and laugh. Amen.

DAY 5: YOURSELF

BE ENTHUSIASTIC.

ENTHUSIASM IS THE most important factor to success and enjoyment in everything. Even if you're doing a task you're not excited about, do it with enthusiasm and it will change your frame of mind and add enjoyment to what you're doing. I have a friend who doesn't like to clean, so she dresses up in a costume to do her house cleaning, which adds to the fun of a not-so-fun task.

The following photos show my daughters helping sell our herbs at the Farmers' Market over 20 years ago. They posed for the one on the left ("Let's look sad to be here."). The one on the right shows their real enthusiasm, which helped pass the time and made it a lot more enjoyable for all of us as well as the customers.

My daughters acting less than enthusias-   Their actual enthusiasm to be with me.
tic to be helping at the Farmers' Market.

"Don't ask what the world needs. Ask what makes you
come alive and go do it, because what the world needs
is more people who have come alive."
~ HOWARD THURMAN

"Nothing great was ever achieved without enthusiasm."
~RALPH WALDO EMERSON (1803-1882)

In the Book of Nehemiah, particularly Chapter 3, Nehemiah enthusiastically rebuilds the wall around Jerusalem:

Nehemiah 2:18 ~ "I told them that the hand of my God had been gracious upon me, and also the words that the king had spoken to me. Then they said, 'Let us start building!' So, they committed themselves to the common good."

Ephesians 6:7 ~ "Render service with enthusiasm, as to the Lord and not to men and women."

Prayer
Creator God,
Direct my enthusiasm in all I do. I can accomplish even an unpleasant task with enthusiasm if I do it in Your name. Amen.

DAY 6: YOURSELF

DO SOMETHING NICE WITHOUT EXPECTING ANYTHING IN RETURN.

MY SISTER SANDY once said, "Sometimes you put into the pool and sometimes you take out." This means sometimes you do something nice for someone (putting into the pool) and other times someone else does something for you (you take out of the pool), not necessarily reciprocating to the same person. It reminds me of when I was a new mom and someone brought me and my family dinner, and down the road, I brought dinner to another new mom and her family. For me, giving is easier than receiving. But if you don't let someone give to you, you are robbing them of the good feeling of doing something nice for others.

> "You were born to make a difference, to contribute
> and to share your gifts with the world."
> ~ DARREN HARDY

> "True happiness comes from a sense of inner peace and
> contentment, which in turn must be achieved through the
> cultivation of altruism, of love and compassion,
> and elimination of ignorance, selfishness, and greed."
> ~ THE DALAI LAMA

Psalm 37:21 ~ "The wicked borrow and do not pay back, but the righteous are generous and keep giving; . . ."

Nehemiah 13:14 ~ "Remember me, O my God, concerning this, and do not wipe out my good deeds that I have done for the house of my God and for his service."

Prayer
Generous God,
Thank You for all You have provided. Direct my path so I can be generous to others. Amen.

DAY 7: YOURSELF

FIND A CAUSE YOU ARE PASSIONATE ABOUT AND DO SOMETHING ABOUT IT.

I AM PASSIONATE about culinary herbs! My passion began in 1980, I grew it into a business in 1983, and the rest is history. I have used herbs every day since.

I would like to share a story of passion with you. It's called "The Starfish Story: One Step Towards Changing the World" by Loren Eiseley (1907-1977).

> *Once upon a time, there was an old man who used to go to the ocean to do his writing. He had a habit of walking on the beach every morning before he began his work. Early one morning, he was walking along the shore after a big storm had passed and found the vast beach littered with starfish as far as the eye could see, stretching in both directions. Off in the distance, the old man noticed a small boy approaching. As the boy walked, he paused every so often and as he grew closer, the man could see that he was occasionally bending down to pick up an object and throw it into the sea.*
>
> *The boy came closer still and the man called out,*

"Good morning! May I ask what it is that you are doing?"

The young boy paused, looked up, and answered, "Throwing starfish into the ocean. The tide has washed them up onto the beach and they can't return to the sea by themselves. When the sun gets high, they will die unless I throw them back into the water."

The old man replied, "But there must be tens of thousands of starfish on this beach. I'm afraid you won't really be able to make much of a difference."

The boy bent down, picked up yet another starfish, and threw it as far as he could into the ocean. Then he turned, smiled, and said, "It made a difference to that one!"[6]

This boy's passion was saving starfish. He was one person following his passion and helping as much as he could. We don't have to save every person to make a difference; just helping one person fulfills that goal. What are you going to do today to make a difference?

"Follow your passion. It will lead you to your purpose."
~ OPRAH WINFREY

"God doesn't just give you resources for your own enjoyment,
but to make a difference in the world around you.
God never blesses us just to sit on what we have.
He blesses us so we can bless others."
~ RICK WARREN

Genesis 39:3 ~ "His master saw that the Lord was with him, and that the Lord caused all that he did to prosper in his hands."

Colossians 3:23 ~ "Whatever your task, put yourselves into it, as done for the Lord and not for your masters."

Prayer
Dear Lord,
Reveal to me my passion so it can make a difference in my life and that of others. Amen.

Reflections from Week 1

1.   The ways to make a difference I liked best this week were:

☐ Day 1   ☐ Day 4   ☐ Day 7
☐ Day 2   ☐ Day 5
☐ Day 3   ☐ Day 6

2.   What kind of tree did you plant? Indoors or outdoors?
3.   When you told someone you were sorry, what was the person's reaction?
4.   What was the reaction of the person you forgave? Were you the one you forgave?
5.   What did you do to make someone laugh? What was their reaction?
6.   What were you enthusiastic about? How did your enthusiasm change your experience?
7.   What nice thing did you do without expecting anything in return? How did that make you feel inside?
8.   What cause are you passionate about? What are you doing about that passion?
9.   Were you inspired to do something additional to or different from the seven items for this week and, if so, what were they? What were the results?
10.   List some of the ways you felt while you were making a difference this week.

DAY 8: YOURSELF

TELL SOMEONE "I WAS WRONG."

WHEN I WAS young, my dad would jokingly say, "I was only wrong once and that was when I thought I was wrong, but I was really right." We knew that wasn't true, and so did he!

When you're wrong, people who were there know you were wrong. By admitting it, you're showing yourself you're brave enough to admit it, and you're showing others you're honest with yourself.

According to neuropsychologist Dr. Sanam Hafeez, "Admitting we are wrong shows others that we are compassionate, empathetic, sympathetic, and good listeners. It also shows that we are capable of being objective about ourselves and that we are not 'perfect' or always right."[7]

" . . . [T]here's a narrow line dividing healthy confidence and stubborn ego, and one of the primary indicators you've landed on the wrong side is not being able to admit when you're wrong."[8]
~ WENDY ROSE GOULD

"If it is challenging to personally take accountability for your mistakes it can be helpful to enlist those relationships in your life that are supportive, caring and willing to help. While it may seem like a really big step to make yourself so vulnerable, just remember how it can open you up to the acceptance and deep emotional connection you need."
~ DR. KATE KAPLAN, LICENSED CLINICAL PSYCHOLOGIST[9]

Numbers 5:7 ~ " . . . and shall confess the sin that has been committed. The person shall make full restitution for the wrong, adding one-fifth to it, and giving it to the one who was wronged."

1 Samuel 26:21 ~ "Then Saul said, 'I have done wrong; come back, my son David, for I will never harm you again, because my life was precious in your sight today; I have been a fool and have made a great mistake.'"

Prayer
Dear Jesus,
I know You did not waste Your time on Earth sacrificing Your life for me. I am not perfect. Help me admit when I am wrong and have the courage to share my imperfections with others. Amen.

DAY 9: YOURSELF

EXERCISE.

WE ALL KNOW exercise is good for us. The Mayo Clinic affirms that regular physical activity . . .

- controls weight,
- combats health conditions and diseases,
- improves mood,
- boosts energy,
- promotes better sleep,
- puts the spark back into your sex life, and
- can be fun—as well as social.

During the pandemic, some gyms were closed so it became more difficult to do certain exercises. However, something simple like walking, stretching, or bike riding can be a positive addition to your life.

My husband Nile going out for a bike ride

"The truth is anyone can be the difference; all it takes is using whatever you have, to do whatever you can."
~ Darius Graham, *Being the Difference*[10]

"Exercise is a celebration of what your body can do.
Not a punishment for what you ate."
~ Anonymous

1 Corinthians 6:19 ~ "Or do you not know that your body is a temple of the Holy Spirit within you, which you have from God, and that you are not your own?"

3 John 1:2 ~ "Beloved, I pray that all may go well with you and that you may be in good health, just as it is well with your soul."

Prayer
Dear Father in Heaven,
Thank You for my body and giving me the blessing of exercise. If I am able, help me get out there and move. Amen.

DAY 10: YOURSELF

CHOOSE JOY.

EVERY MORNING YOU can decide to choose joy! Some days it seems difficult to make that choice, but it is always a choice. Choose joy today!

Getting out in nature brings me joy. I love walking around looking at all that God has created.

Activities that promote joy can be as simple as listening to music or doing something new. If you aren't feeling joyful, do things with joyful people and that will promote joy in you.

Bella, my four-year-old granddaughter

This photo displays the joy of my granddaughter Bella, alone with her mom and dad in church because her three older siblings had gone to Sunday school. This was the first time she had attended church instead of Sunday school and being there with the music and alone with her mom and dad was a joyful time for her.

Like Bella, choose joy! It can make a difference in and for you.

"Every morning is an opportunity to choose joy!"
~ CHARLES SWINDOLL

"Joy is the simplest form of gratitude."
~ Karl Barth, theologian (1886-1968)

Job 8:21 ~ "He will yet fill your mouth with laughter, and your lips with shouts of joy."

Psalm 65:8 ~ "Those who live at earth's farthest bounds are awed by your signs; you make the gateways of the morning and the evening shout for joy."

Prayer
Joyful Savior,
My true joy is in You. Help me discover the joy You have put everywhere for me to find so I choose joy every day. Amen.

DAY 11: YOURSELF

SPEND 15-30 MINUTES IN COMPLETE SOLITUDE.

When my kids were young, having a moment of solitude was an unattainable dream. One time I told one of my daughters I would pay her a penny for every minute she was quiet. It was the best 45 cents I ever spent! Just having it quiet for three quarters of an hour helped me get my thoughts together.

Solitude can give you the ability to hear your thoughts, which allows for making better decisions and listening to your intuition. You need to reach the understanding that God is in charge, not you or anyone else. This should relieve the stress and lift the burdens of the world from your shoulders. Solitude gives you a chance to turn your burdens over to God, meditate, and receive His insights. Time by yourself gives you clarity to make a difference in your own life and then in others.

"A little while alone in your room will prove more valuable than anything else that could ever be given you."
~ THE ESSENTIAL RUMI

"True peace with oneself and with the world around us can only be achieved through the development of mental peace."
~ THE DALAI LAMA

Matthew 13:14 ~ "Now when Jesus heard this, he withdrew from there in a boat to a deserted place by himself. But when the crowds heard it, they followed him on foot from the towns."

John 6:15 ~ "When Jesus realized that they were about to come and take him by force to make him king, he withdrew again to the mountain by himself."

Prayer
Loving God,
Thank You for speaking to me in solitude. In the quiet moments, I can hear in my mind the wee small voice as I follow Your example for quiet. Amen.

DAY 12: YOURSELF

TAKE TIME TO PRAY FOR YOUR NEEDS.

I HAVE ALWAYS found prayer to be a real comfort. There have been times that I did not understand the answer to my prayers, but that is very human.

Linda Canup quotes Dr. Charles Stanley of Intouch Ministries: ". . . [P]rayer helps us be wise stewards of time because it . . .

1. provides timely direction,
2. prevents wrong decisions,
3. eliminates worry and anxiety,
4. produces peacefulness,

5.   invites God into our activity,
6.   generates confidence,
7.   eliminates fretting,
8.   sharpens discernment,
9.   gives us energy,
10. prevents distractions,
11. reminds us to act now,
12. protects us from discouragement,
13. opens doors of opportunity, and
14. helps us discern between busyness and fruitfulness."[11]

We could all benefit from at least one of the items listed. Spend time in prayer today and see how it makes a difference.

"I used to believe that prayer changes things, but now I know that prayer changes us, and He changes things."
~ MOTHER TERESA (1910-1997)

"Help me to see the potential You see in others. And speaking of potential, allow me to see my own unique potential for making a positive difference in my world."
~ LEE WISE

Matthew 7:7 ~ "Ask, and it will be given you; search, and you will find; knock, and the door will be opened for you."

Matthew 26:39 ~ "And going a little farther, he threw himself on the ground and prayed, "My Father, if it is possible, let this cup pass from me; yet not what I want but what you want."

Prayer
Ever-Present Lord,
Thank You for always being awake to hear my prayers. Whether it is in the middle of the night or the busyness of the day, You never sleep so You are always there giving me direction. Help me to hear You. Amen.

DAY 13: YOURSELF

SHARE SOME EXTRA GARDEN PRODUCE.

DURING GARDENING SEASON, those of you with vegetable gardens often have extra. A great thing to do is to share the extra with any of the following:

1. Family
2. Friends
3. Neighbors
4. Church members
5. Mail carrier
6. Local soup kitchen
7. Local food pantry

We want to be good stewards of all things, including extra produce. With many people in need of food, sharing blesses both our souls and theirs, as well as their bodies.

Just growing things boosts my spirits, but sharing my harvest makes me feel even better! We have grown currants for 30 years, and I made currant jelly from them this year. One day my mail carrier, Cathy, came by, and I gave her a letter that I'd gotten by mistake. She recognized the address and said, "That's from Riverside. Those people were displaced because of the flood. I have many of those on my route, and I deliver their mail to where they're staying in the interim." I thought it was wonderful that she was going out of her way to do that. I asked her to wait a minute, and I went in and got a jar of jelly to give her as a thank you and to reward her for her thoughtfulness.

Cathy, my mail delivery person, holding
a jar of currant jelly I made and gave her

In the fall, we usually have an abundance of apples, which my husband picks. He polishes each one and puts them in a box. He writes on the box what kind of apple is inside and what to use it for, and then Hidden Harvest comes and picks up the boxes he packed just for them. The apples then get distributed to different food pantries and soup kitchens. He told me when he does this, "I feel great!"

"Never forget to recognize and express gratitude in your life for all the people that make a big difference in your life, for people like your mailperson, your doctor, your newspaper deliverer, etc. Just expressing a 'thank you' is very simple but very powerful!"
~ Catherine Pulsifer

"The people who give you their food give you their heart."
~ Cesar Chavez (1927-1993)

Matthew 25:34-35 ~ "Then the king will say to those at his right hand, 'Come, you that are blessed by my Father, inherit the kingdom prepared for you from the foundation of the world; for I was hungry and you gave me food, I was thirsty and you gave me something to drink, I was a stranger and you welcomed me, . . .'"

Luke 3:11 ~ "In reply he said to them, 'Whoever has two coats must share with anyone who has none; and whoever has food must do likewise.'"

Prayer
God of abundance,
Thank You for Your gifts. Help us remember to share our abundance with those in need. Amen.

DAY 14: YOURSELF

ENCOURAGE A CHILD TO DRAW.

SOME OF THE benefits of drawing for children include the following:

1. **Eye-hand coordination.** Coordination between hands and eyes allow completion of the most ordinary everyday tasks, and practice improves how the eyes and hands work together. If we improve coordination in children, they will have fewer problems in many areas of life. Drawing may seem simple, but it's a big help in developing fine motor skills.
2. **Expression.** Children, especially young ones, don't have the vocabulary to express their wants or feelings, which can be frustrating to them. With a simple drawing, they can show their happiness, sadness, excitement, and so on with just a few simple figures, shapes, lines, and color selection. With practice, their drawing skills will improve, followed by their vocabulary.
3. **Imagination.** Observing an object, character, or situation and studying it carefully can help develop a child's imagination and creativity.

4. **Fun.** It's fun to draw with a child and good for both of you. The time spent with a child is never wasted and can be beneficial for your mental health as well as theirs.

My granddaughter Keagan, drawing a picture for me

"I am only one, but still, I am one. I cannot do everything,
but still, I can do something; and because I cannot do everything,
I will not refuse to do something I can do."
~ Edward Everett Hale

"What you do in life does make a difference to you
and those people who look up to you."
~ Joseph Woodley, *No Generals in the House*

Romans 15:5 ~ "May the God of steadfastness and encouragement grant you to live in harmony with one another, in accordance with Christ Jesus."

I Thessalonians 5:11 ~ "Therefore encourage one another and build up each other, as indeed you are doing."

Prayer
God the Creator,
Thank You for giving me so many ways to express myself, drawing
being one of them. Amen.

Reflections from Week 2

1.   The ways to make a difference I liked best this week were:

☐ Day 8   ☐ Day 11   ☐ Day 14
☐ Day 9   ☐ Day 12
☐ Day 10   ☐ Day 13

2.   When you told someone you were wrong, what was their reaction? Did it take courage on your part?
3.   How did you feel after you exercised? Were you encouraged to continue exercising?
4.   What did you say to yourself to choose joy? What things did you do? How did your choice influence the rest of the day?
5.   Was it difficult to spend time in complete solitude? Write down some of your thoughts while you were in solitude. Did you solve a problem?
6.   Write down some of the needs you have for which you prayed. Did you share those needs with someone?
7.   What do you have growing in your garden that you shared with others? How did that make you feel?
8.   Do you have children in your life that you could encourage to draw? How did you encourage them?
9.   Were you inspired to do something additional to or different from the seven items for this week and, if so, what were they?
10. List some of the ways you felt while you were making a difference for yourself this week.

DAY 15: YOURSELF

PRAY FOR GUIDANCE FOR YOURSELF.

WE ALL HAVE decisions to make every day. Some are easy, such as what to have for breakfast. Others are more difficult, such as deciding if you should send your child to kindergarten this year or wait another year. Our current social climate requires many difficult decisions.

In prayer, we can ask God for wisdom, guidance, clarity, and direction for those confusing and troubled times when we need counsel. We can depend on God for all those things as believers, asking in our daily prayers for direction in our changing times. We pray daily because we make decisions daily, and as we stand at crossroads, our need for direction is even greater. God, being the Higher Power, will guide us in going the right direction, avoiding unforeseen traps along the way. In Him, our victory is sure.

Take time today to pray for guidance, for it will make a difference in yourself.

"Mindset means the way you choose to look at the things coming on their way. But this simple personal philosophy or way of looking at the thing is the single most important factor to make all the difference, whether you live an average or mediocre life or you can leave a legacy behind you."[12]
~ SOM BATHLA, *THE MINDSET MAKEOVER*

"Prayer is man's greatest power."
~ W. CLEMENT STONE (1902-2002)

Proverbs 1:5 ~ "[L]et the wise listen and add to their learning, and let the discerning get guidance . . ."

I Kings 8:59 ~ "And may these words of mine, which I have prayed before the Lord, be near to the Lord our God day and night, that he may uphold the cause of his servant and the cause of his people Israel according to each day's need."

Prayer

Dear God,

I come to You today to ask for wisdom, guidance, clarity, and direction so I can make the right decisions and honor You. Amen.

DAY 16: YOURSELF

SING A SONG AS IF NO ONE IS LISTENING.

SINGING OFFERS MANY health and other benefits.

Singing . . .

1.   boosts the immune system;
2.   can be excellent exercise for everyone, young and old, ill or healthy, because it's a workout for your lungs and diaphragm;
3.   improves posture;
4.   helps strengthen throat and palate muscles, reducing snoring and sleep apnea so you can get a better night's sleep;
5.   is a natural antidepressant;
6.   is relaxing because singing loud and forcefully releases stored muscle tension and dramatically decreases the levels of the stress hormone cortisol in your bloodstream;
7.   improves mental alertness;
8.   boosts your confidence;
9.   broadens your communication skills;
10. increases your ability to appreciate other singers.[13]

So, choose your favorite song from your favorite artist and belt it out. You'll be glad you did! I have done this many times. One time, the family was gone and I was singing loudly when the neighborhood kids came to the door looking for my kids. They rang the doorbell, which I didn't hear, and then said, "She's singing in there!" Indeed, I *was* singing in there—and was happier for it.

"Music has healing power. It has the ability to take people
out of themselves for a few hours."
~ ELTON JOHN

"Singing connects the mind with the heart and the heart
with the soul. So sing. I dare you!"
~ NEALE DONALD WALSCH

Psalm 5:11 ~ "But let all who take refuge in you be glad; let them
ever sing for joy. Spread your protection over them, that those who
love your name may rejoice in you."

Zephaniah 3:14 ~ "Sing, Daughter Zion; shout aloud, Israel! Be
glad and rejoice with all your heart, Daughter Jerusalem!"

Prayer
Lord of expression,
Thank You for the gift of music and song. Singing Your praises is a
way to express my gratitude for not only music but all the gifts You
have given me. Amen.

DAY 17: YOURSELF

GO ON A NATURE WALK, APPRECIATING ALL OF GOD'S CREATIONS.

TAKING A WALK in nature doesn't require a nature preserve; just
be outside in nature where trees and plants are growing, and the
air is fresh.

The Energy Blog gives six reasons to take a walk in nature. A
20-minute walk can reduce stress, which in turn can lower blood
pressure. Being around trees improves your overall mental health
and helps your brain function more clearly with improved concentration and sharper thinking. And most importantly, it gives you a
more positive outlook on life.[14]

Here are a few additional ideas from Sarah of "How Wee Learn." Nature . . .

1. improves immune functioning,
2. improves memory,
3. nurtures creativity, and
4. helps you sleep better.[15]

No matter what the weather, dress appropriately for it and take a walk every day to make a difference in yourself.

Taking a walk in nature with some of my grandchildren

"Taking a walk in nature has healing power for our minds and souls. We don't ask anything from nature, yet nature gives us silence, peace, harmony, and beauty, without limits. Walking in nature is free and efficient therapy for our stressed, fast-paced lives."
~ Mark Centino

"Walk as if you are kissing the Earth with your feet."
~ Vietnamese monk Thich Nhat Hanh (1926-2022), *Peace Is Every Step*

Genesis 13:17 ~ "Go, walk through the length and breadth of the land, for I am giving it to you."

Romans 1:20 ~ "For since the creation of the world God's invisible qualities—his eternal power and divine nature—have been clearly seen, being understood from what has been made, so that people are without excuse."

Prayer
Powerful God,
You created our world with just Your words. Help me get out in nature to enjoy and be thankful for Your creation. Amen.

DAY 18: YOURSELF

EAT NUTRITIOUS FOODS.

VISIT YOUR FARMERS' Market when fresh produce is abundant—fruits and vegetables of all kinds! We all know we are supposed to eat plenty of fruits and vegetables, but what exactly do they do for us?

According to Amanda Hernandez, a registered dietitian, fruits and vegetables . . .

1. are full of the essential nutrients you need. Fruit is naturally low in fat, sodium, and calories, and rich in potassium, fiber, vitamin C, and folate;
2. have fiber that helps to protect against heart disease and lower cholesterol;.
3. help protect eye health;
4. help with disease prevention; (Eating produce can cut your risk of cardiovascular disease, stroke, and type 2 diabetes and protect against various forms of cancer.)
5. help with weight management;
6. help balance the pH of your body (its acidity and alkalinity);

7.   help keep your mind sharp.[16]

So, when your body and mind are taken care of, the rest falls into place. My dad would ask us, "If you don't take care of your body, where are you going to live?" Take good care of yourself by eating some fresh fruits and vegetables today.

Fresh produce at the Farmers' Market

"Our food should be our medicine and our
medicine should be our food."
~ HIPPOCRATES (460-370 BC)

"If we take good care of ourselves, we help everyone."
THICH NHAT HANH (1926-2022), *How to Love*

Exodus 23:25 ~ "Worship the Lord your God, and his blessing will be on your food and water. I will take away sickness from among you."

Psalm 104:14 ~ "He makes grass grow for the cattle, and plants for people to cultivate—bringing forth food from the earth."

Prayer
Great provider,
You have supplied all that my body needs. Help me to choose foods that nourish me and make me a healthier person to do Your work. Amen.

READ A BOOK.

I HAVE DONE a lot of reading for information, but about 15 years ago I began reading for pleasure, which has added richly to my life.

According to Catherine Winter on LifeHack, reading offers at least 10 benefits:

1. **Mental stimulation** ~ This can slow the progress of (or possibly even prevent) Alzheimer's and dementia.
2. **Stress reduction** ~ Lose yourself in a book and melt away the stress of the day.
3. **Knowledge** ~ Everything you read fills your head with new bits of information, and you never know when it might come in handy. The more knowledge you have, the better equipped you are to tackle any challenge you'll ever face. In addition, should you ever find yourself in dire circumstances, remember that although you might lose everything else—your job, your possessions, your money, even your health—knowledge can never be taken from you.
4. **Vocabulary expansion** ~ The more you read, the more words you gain exposure to, and they'll inevitably make their way into your everyday vocabulary.
5. **Memory improvement** ~ When you read a fiction book or memoir, you have to remember an assortment of characters, their backgrounds, ambitions, history, and nuances, as well as the various arcs and subplots that weave their way through every story. That's a fair bit to remember,

but brains are marvelous things and can remember these things with relative ease.

6. **Stronger analytical thinking skills** ~ These skills come into play particularly if you are reading a mystery and trying to discover "whodunnit."

7. **Improved focus and concentration** ~ When you read a book, all of your attention is focused on the story as the rest of the world just falls away, and you can immerse yourself in every fine detail you're absorbing.

8. **Better writing skills** ~ Exposure to published, well-written work has a noted effect on one's own writing, as observing the cadence, fluidity, and writing styles of other authors will invariably influence your own work.

9. **Tranquility** ~ Reading spiritual texts can lower blood pressure and bring about an immense sense of calm. Reading self-help books has been shown to help people suffering from certain mood disorders and mild mental illnesses.

10. **Free entertainment** ~ For low-budget entertainment, you can visit your local library and bask in the glory of the countless tomes available there for free. Libraries have books on every subject imaginable, and since they rotate their stock and constantly get new books, you'll never run out of reading materials.[17]

So, on this 19th day of your Make a Difference journey, make a difference in yourself by picking up a book and reading it!

The bookshelves in my office

"From the reading of 'good books' there comes a
richness of life that can be obtained in no other way."
~ Gordon B. Hinckley

"A house without books is like a room without windows."
~ Horace Mann (1933-2021)

Deuteronomy 17:19 ~ "It is to be with him, and he is to read it all
the days of his life so that he may learn to revere the Lord his God
and follow carefully all the words of this law and these decrees."

Acts 8:28 ~ ". . . and on his way home was sitting in his chariot
reading the Book of Isaiah the prophet."

Prayer
God of words,
Thank You for books, particularly the Bible. Help me find time to
read from Your Word and other books You led people to write. They
hold answers. Amen.

DO SOMETHING THAT LIFTS YOUR SPIRITS.

EACH OF US has things or activities that lift our spirits, and during this time of unrest in the world, we're in need of a lift more than usual. A lot of the suggestions listed for the previous 19 days can lift your spirits, and here are additional ways offered by Corina Semph on the Tiny Buddha blog:

1. Buy yourself a bouquet or pick one from your garden.
2. Write down the people and things for which you're grateful.
3. Pamper yourself with a massage, manicure, or pedicure.
4. Take an hour and go through some old stuff and get rid of what you aren't using anymore.
5. Find a space and make it into a place of peace. You can decorate it with flowers, candles, and peaceful pictures and colors.
6. Avoid negative people and influences and surround yourself with positive ones.
7. Set limits for yourself. You only have so much time in a day. If you say yes to something, you are also saying no to something else that may be even more important.
8. Make someone else happy, which will also make you happy.
9. Become a recovering perfectionist. No one is perfect. Lifting the burden of trying to be will lift your spirits.
10. Make time for a good friend. Spending time with friends is invaluable.
11. Look at your positive traits. Dig deep and remind yourself of your special abilities and characteristics.[18]
12. Listen to cheerful, upbeat music.

"True happiness is born of letting go of what is unnecessary."
~ SHARON SALZBERG

"Happiness cannot be traveled to, owned, earned, worn,
or consumed. Happiness is the spiritual experience of
living every minute with love, grace, and gratitude."
~ DENIS WAITLEY

Psalm 37:4 ~ "Take delight in the Lord, and he will give you the desires of your heart."

Matthew 25:21 ~ "His master replied, 'Well done, good and faithful servant! You have been faithful with a few things; I will put you in charge of many things. Come and share your master's happiness!'"

Prayer
Awesome God,
Help me find the positives in the way You made me. Lift my spirits so I can "praise you, for I am fearfully and wonderfully made. Wonderful are your works; that I know very well" (Psalm 139: 14). Amen.

DAY 21: YOURSELF

THINK ABOUT THINGS YOU WOULD CHANGE.

I USUALLY DON'T advocate having regrets, but we all have at least one thing we would like to do over and do better. That said, we can learn from some regrets and make changes in our here and now to end those regrets. Even everybody's friend Erma Bombeck—the gal you'd think never regretted a moment—agreed.

One of our favorites ~ Erma Bombeck

She admitted:

If I had my life to live over again, I would have waxed less and listened more. Instead of wishing away nine months of pregnancy and complaining about the shadows over my feet, I'd have cherished every minute of it and realized that the wonderment growing inside me was to be my only chance in life to assist God in a miracle. . . . I would have cried and laughed less while watching television . . . and more while watching life. . . . There would have been more I love yous . . . more I'm sorrys . . . more I'm listening . . . but mostly, given another shot at life, I would seize every minute of it . . . and never give that minute back until there was nothing left of it.[19]

"Life can only be understood backwards;
but it must be lived forwards."
~ SOREN KIERKEGAARD

Philippians 3:13-15 ~ "Beloved, I do not consider that I have made it my own; but this one thing I do: forgetting what lies behind and straining forward to what lies ahead, I press on toward the goal for the prize of the heavenly call of God in Christ Jesus. Let those of us then who are mature be of the same mind; and if you think differently about anything, this too God will reveal to you."

Galatians 4:20 ~ ". . . how I wish I could be with you now and change my tone, because I am perplexed about you!"

Prayer
Lord of Heaven and Earth,
Thank You for encouraging me to make a difference in myself. I want to follow Your ways and be an example to others. Amen.

Reflections from Week 3

1. The ways to make a difference I liked best this week were:

    ☐ Day 15   ☐ Day 18   ☐ Day 21
    ☐ Day 16   ☐ Day 19
    ☐ Day 17   ☐ Day 20

2. Are you struggling to decide which way to go? Did you pray for guidance? What was the response?
3. What song did you choose to belt out? How did it feel?
4. What did you see on your nature walk? Are you encouraged to walk more often?
5. Did you make good nutritious foods on Day 18? What did you eat?
6. What book did you decide to read? What genre was it? Were you familiar with the author?
7. What lifted your spirits? Have you ever used that item or done that activity before? Where was your temperament before you began and where was it after you did it?
8. Do you live with regrets? How can you change those things from a negative to a positive and look forwards instead of backwards?
9. Were you inspired to do something additional to the seven items for this week and, if so, what were they?
10. List some of the ways you felt while you were making a difference this week.

This is the last day of Make a Difference in Yourself. For the next 17 days, we will look at Make a Difference in Your Family. I encourage you to continue reading and doing the things I suggest or something of your own inspiration. Your results will further support your actions.

CHAPTER 2

MAKE A DIFFERENCE IN YOUR FAMILY

As YOU LOOK at the ripples in the pond, they are deeper and stronger in the center than the ones that radiate outward. Now we will move outward on the ripples of influence to our family, taking our enthusiasm, direction, and refreshed spirit along with us.

Making a difference in your family can be a complicated thing. If you are a parent of small children, you are the strongest influence in their lives. You can touch them with your ripples, which will encourage them to create their own ripples, influencing others in a positive way, following God's desires for our lives.

Why Make a Difference in Your Family?
Six good reasons are to:

1. show them you love them;
2. make the family unit stronger;
3. build their confidence;
4. make society a better place in which to live;
5. be a role model for random acts of kindness;
6. help create a better future for the world.

TELL EACH OF YOUR CHILDREN AND/ OR GRANDCHILDREN YOU LOVE THEM.

THE ACT OF verbalizing your love to family members does a lot for them. You don't know if you will have another chance to tell them because life is short and you don't know what tomorrow will bring. Also:

1. You don't know what kind of a day they are having, and telling someone you love them can make a big difference in how the rest of their day goes.
2. You could regret not telling them. Don't live with regrets.
3. What you say can be contagious so you could be the initiator for uplifting many people.
4. It is reassuring for our family to know that we love them and cherish them. It gives purpose to their lives.
5. Sophie Martin said, "The older we get, the more clear it becomes that loving and being loved are the only really important things in life. The rest is kind of just filler."[20]

"Grandparents are living longer, doing more, and refusing to accept any limitations. But they still make a difference, one at a time, for their grandchildren."
~ JACK CANFIELD, CHICKEN SOUP FOR THE GRANDPARENT'S SOUL

"Love isn't a state of perfect caring. It is an active noun like 'struggle.' To love someone is to strive to accept that person exactly the way he or she is, right here and now."
~ MR. (FRED) ROGERS (1928-2003)

Psalm 103:17 ~ "But the steadfast love of the Lord is from everlasting to everlasting on those who fear him, and his righteousness to children's children, ..."

John 13:34 ~ "I give you a new commandment, that you love one another. Just as I have loved you, you also should love one another."

Prayer
Dear Father,
Your love is an example to us all. Help us verbalize and share our love with our family members. Amen.

DAY 2 (23 overall): FAMILY

ENCOURAGE A FAMILY MEMBER, VERBALLY OR WITH A WRITTEN NOTE.

DEPENDING ON YOUR family dynamics, this can be easy or extremely complicated. The term "family dynamics" refers to the ways in which family members relate to and interact with one another. These relationships are in constant flux because experiences continue to be added to each of our lives.

I consider this ongoing change positive. If the people within the family change, so can the way we relate to one another. A simple phone call or note of encouragement can change that relationship for the better. If using your voice doesn't seem right for you, write a note. A note can be less threatening because it's a one-way conversation. By encouraging that family member, you can make a difference in their life. Take the first step. Remember, you can always write to more than one person.

> "If there was ever a time to dare, to make a difference,
> to embark on something worth doing, IT IS NOW."
> ~ AUTHOR UNKNOWN

> "As human beings, our job in life is to help people realize
> how rare and valuable each one of us really is, that each of us
> has something that no one else has or ever will have,
> something inside that is unique to all time."
> ~ MR. (FRED) ROGERS (1928-2003)

Job 16:5 ~ "I could encourage you with my mouth, and the solace of my lips would assuage your pain."

Galatians 5:25 ~ "If we live by the Spirit, let us also be guided by the Spirit."

Prayer
Transforming God,
Thank You for caring enough about us to transform us and our relationships so the family unit is preserved. Give us the words to say to make a difference in others' lives. Amen.

DAY 3 (24 overall): FAMILY

BE ENTHUSIASTIC ABOUT A FAMILY MEMBER'S PROJECT.

It doesn't matter how old or young your family members are, someone always seems to be working on a project. It can be as simple as a 50-piece jigsaw puzzle or as complicated as a 1,000-piece Lego set for building a three-dimensional replica of the White House. It could be a school project, a work project, a home project, or a church project, to name a few. Whatever it is, a little encouragement and enthusiasm give new energy to the person tackling the project at hand. You can lift them over a hump when they're struggling with what to do next, or your enthusiasm can encourage them to finish. Being a successful leader sets an example for others to follow, and they will work harder because of your enthusiasm.

> "If we did all the things we are capable of,
> we would astound ourselves."
> ~ Thomas Edison (1847-1931)

"Mutual caring relationships require kindness and patience, tolerance, optimism, joy in the other's achievements, confidence in oneself, and the ability to give without undue thought of gain."
~ MR. (FRED) ROGERS (1928-2003)

Isaiah 41:10 ~ "Do not fear, for I am with you, do not be afraid, for I am your God; I will strengthen you, I will help you, I will uphold you with my victorious right hand."

1 Thessalonians 5:11 ~ "Therefore encourage one another and build up each other, as indeed you are doing."

Prayer
Encouraging God,
Help us to encourage others as You encourage us. We want to reflect Your image and who You are. Amen.

DAY 4 (25 overall): FAMILY

GET DOWN ON THE FLOOR AND PLAY WITH YOUR CHILDREN, GRANDCHILDREN, OR NIECES AND NEPHEWS.

MY SISTER KAREN, who passed away in 2014, had three grandsons that she loved dearly. She told me once, "I am the grandma who gets down on the floor and plays with my grandkids."

That made me decide, "I want to be that grandma!" So, I got down on the floor and played. The older I get, the more difficult it is to get down and even more difficult to get up, but to the kids it's the best thing I can do. I'm down on their level, interested in what they are doing and having great interaction with them. My grandkids and I raced Hot Wheels cars back and forth. We also put together floor puzzles and played with a Barbie Doll Playhouse.

The important thing is not what you do, it is that you do it. They will remember that you were "that grandma."

When we play with our grandkids, it's a two-way street of benefits. We both develop patience and get in touch with how the other behaves in these situations. As grandparents, our expectations are different from those of their parents. With mutual respect, affection, and understanding of what we can teach and learn from one another, we can teach and learn things we can't anywhere else, showing them the beginning of selfless behavior.[21]

As grandparents, we can most likely devote more time than parents, which adds to the children's feelings of safety and stability. Also, grandparents have different life experiences than parents, which give children a wider view of life. In return, children can give grandparents a purpose, which can minimize depression by increasing social connection.[22] So, get down on the floor, even if you need help getting up!

"By giving up a little portion of your life, by letting go of your selfishness, you can make a big difference in some lives."
~ Henry Cloud and John Townsend, Boundaries

"Time spent playing with children is never wasted."
~ Dawn Lantero

Matthew 18:2-4 ~ "He called a child, whom he put among them, and said, 'Truly I tell you, unless you change and become like children, you will never enter the kingdom of heaven. Whoever becomes humble like this child is the greatest in the kingdom of heaven.'"

Psalm 127:3 ESV ~ "Behold, children are a heritage from the Lord, the fruit of the womb a reward."

Prayer
Parent of us all,
We ask You to bless our interactions with people of all ages. We can learn from one another and share the gifts You have given us. Amen.

DAY 5 (26 overall): FAMILY

LISTEN TO WHAT OTHERS SAY.

WITH OUR FAST-PACED lives, we each have an agenda or are on a schedule that doesn't lend itself to good listening skills.

Sometimes I find myself almost as if I had blinders on, heading straight ahead with what's on my mind, skipping the social pleasantries that should be exchanged before anything else. That can lead people to think I'm not interested in what they have to say and I'm too regimented to care about them.

Families are the testing ground for social behaviors we should use outside of the family unit. Start first with your family by listening to them. You may learn a lot about them and how they feel about the world and their place in it.

By listening to others, you help them feel valued by showing compassion and understanding. But you can also learn how they feel about different subjects, which develops patience and the ability to be more tolerant.[23]

So, during the next small talk you have, try to stop thinking, eliminate shyness and all the barriers between you, close your mouth, and just listen. Others don't always need you to fix the situation; they just want to be heard.

"Attentive listening to others lets them know that you love them and builds trust, the foundation of a loving relationship."
~ BRIAN TRACY

"Listen to others without judging. All people have the right to believe whatever they want to believe; they have the right to say whatever they want to say. Instead of judging what other people say, listen and show your respect."
~ DON MIGUEL RUIZ

Proverbs 2:2 ~ "Making your ear attentive to wisdom and inclining your heart to understanding; . . ."

James 1:19 ~ "You must understand this, my beloved: let everyone be quick to listen, slow to speak, slow to anger; . . ."

Prayer
Compassionate God,
You gave us one mouth and two ears. Help us to listen twice as much as we speak, showing Your compassion to others. Amen.

DAY 6 (27 overall): FAMILY

ASK FOR OR GIVE FORGIVENESS.

ASKING FOR FORGIVENESS is one of the most difficult things to do because of fear of what the other person will or will not say. But, depending on the transgression, forgiving someone else can also be difficult. We must remember, none of us are perfect. We all have done things to hurt someone else, and likewise, others have done hurtful things to us. Holding those hurts in or stewing about what you did wrong is not good for your health.

Byron Katie reminds us, "Forgiveness is just another name for freedom." That freedom can reduce our stress thus lowering our heart rate and blood pressure, which is a benefit we all could use. Holding on to unforgiveness adds to anger, depression, and anxiety. Forgiveness shows compassion and helps us let go of hostility, giving us an improved and happier well-being with healthier and more plentiful relationships.[24]

Whether you've chosen a religion or not, forgiveness will bring you closer to Spirit. When we ask God for help and offer our fear, sadness, and pain as a prayer, we receive peace and divine love in return. This is true healing.

"Forgiveness does not change the past,
but it does enlarge the future."
~ PAUL LEWIS BOESE (1923-1976)

"To err is human, to forgive divine."
~ ALEXANDER POPE (1688-1744)

Luke 6:37 ~ "Do not judge, and you will not be judged; do not condemn, and you will not be condemned. Forgive, and you will be forgiven; . . ."

Ephesians 4:32 ~ ". . . [B]e kind to one another, tenderhearted, forgiving one another, as God in Christ has forgiven you."

Prayer
Healing God,
Help me to forgive and be forgiven. Please take away my sadness, anger, and pain and turn it into peace and love for the ones I have hurt and the ones who have hurt me. Amen.

DAY 7 (28 overall): FAMILY

GO ON A DATE WITH YOUR SPOUSE, SIGNIFICANT OTHER, OR FRIEND.

DATE NIGHT IS not just for married couples. With all that was and is going on with COVID-19, we need social contact more than ever, whether that is with a spouse, a significant other, or a friend. We need time without our phone, television, computer, and to-do list. We need time to socialize and for real conversations—words spoken in person, not written or spoken on a television. You can go out to dinner and try a new restaurant or a new food or bring your own food for a picnic to save money.

This close one-on-one interaction can reignite your relationship. It also gives you a chance to share what's on your mind, both the positive and the negative. The other person can do the same, which gives you an opportunity to focus on someone else—to share their burdens, give advice, or just listen. This can give you a lift that's much needed right now. You'll know you aren't alone with how you are currently feeling, and it gives you a chance to understand someone else's concerns. All of this builds a stronger bond between the two of you. If you're focused on each other, there's no room to be focused on someone else.

"A successful marriage requires falling in love many times, always with the same person."
~ Mignon McLaughlin (1913-1983)

"Friendship is born at that moment when one person says to another, 'What! You too? I thought I was the only one.'"
~ C. S. Lewis (1898-1963)

John 13:35 ~ "By this everyone will know that you are my disciples, if you have love for one another."

Proverbs 17:17 ~ "A friend loves at all times, . . ."

Prayer
Jesus, our Lord and Savior,
You blessed our relationship. Please bless our time together so it's productive and nurturing. Amen.

Reflections From Week 4

1. The ways to make a difference I liked best this week were:

    ☐ Day 22   ☐ Day 25   ☐ Day 28
    ☐ Day 23   ☐ Day 26
    ☐ Day 24   ☐ Day 27

2. How did you tell them you loved them—on the phone, in an email, with a handwritten note? How did they react?
3. What family member did you encourage and how did you do it?
4. What was the project and who was working on it?
5. Who did you play with and did you really get down on the floor? Could you get back up again?
6. How are your listening skills? Did they improve after this exercise? What would you do differently next time?
7. Now that you have forgiven yourself, is it easier to forgive someone else? Did you give or get forgiveness?
8. Who was the person on the date? Where did you go on your date? Was the alone time beneficial? Did you choose a day for your next date?
9. Were you inspired to do some things additional to the seven items for this week, and if so, what were they?
10. List some of the ways you felt while you were making a difference this week.

DAY 8 (29 overall): FAMILY

SPEND SOME ONE-ON-ONE TIME WITH EACH OF YOUR KIDS, GRANDKIDS, AND/OR NIECES AND NEPHEWS.

SPENDING TIME ONE on one out of the house gives you a chance to focus on each child separately. It reinforces that you love them and think they are special. No matter what age they are, it builds a close relationship that lasts a lifetime. Because you are busy and the kids know this, it makes an even bigger impact that you're taking time just for them.

The conversations you have during this "date" benefit you as well. You get to know your child's heart and what's on their mind. They get to see you in a different environment and observe how you act. This sets guidelines for how they should act on a date. You're also making a difference in other parents' lives by setting a great example they could emulate. Keep it simple and just "talk, laugh, cry, agree, disagree, and always part ways with an 'I love you.'"[25]

When my oldest was in middle school, a nearby corner store offered great homemade pizza. Periodically, after I picked her up from school, we would go there for a small pizza. It was a perfect time to visit and have a good conversation.

Your visits don't need to be expensive or time consuming. A half-hour date for an ice cream cone or a smoothie can give you insight into your child that you wouldn't get any other way.

If you're lucky, you'll be rewarded with priceless feedback. The other day I was talking with my five-year-old granddaughter on the phone and she said, "Mimi, I love you from the bottom of my heart." It doesn't get any better than that!

"Spending TIME with children is more important
than spending MONEY on children."
~ ANTHONY DOUGLAS WILLIAMS

"I have created nothing really beautiful, really lasting, but if I can inspire one of these youngsters to develop the talent I know they possess, then my monument will be in their work."
~ AUGUSTA SAVAGE (1892-1962)

Deuteronomy 12:28 ~ "Be careful to obey all these words that I command you today, so that it may go well with you and with your children after you forever, because you will be doing what is good and right in the sight of the Lord your God."

1 Corinthians 16:7 ~ "I do not want to see you now just in passing, for I hope to spend some time with you, if the Lord permits."

Prayer
O Lord Jesus,
Help us remember how important it is to spend time with each other one on one. Give us the time and the desire to reconnect with the people we love. Amen.

DAY 9 (30 overall): FAMILY

HELP A FAMILY MEMBER CLEAN THEIR HOUSE OR GARDEN.

NO MATTER WHAT age someone is, they could use some help cleaning. It could be an older family member who can't do what they used to, whether it's cleaning their house or weeding and pruning their garden. It could be one of your family members who's sick, has just had surgery, or has had a baby and needs your help. Or it could be a young child who needs help cleaning their room. Whatever the situation, another set of hands is always welcome.

Your help could encourage someone when they look out and see the garden in which they took so much pride looking like it used to—well-kept and beautiful. A clean kitchen or bathroom could lift the spirits of someone recovering from a stay in the hospital who doesn't have the strength to clean it themselves.

Helping and showing a young child how to clean their room teaches them how to do it themselves. Your help gets them over the hump of cleaning an overwhelmingly big mess.

Our youngest daughter has caught the gardening bug but is not yet knowledgeable, so we have gone to her house several times to help weed, put in gardens, prune, plant, and teach. To work alongside a knowledgeable person, teaches and encourages, and gets the job down to a manageable level.

"Small acts of kindness can make a difference in other people's lives more than we can imagine."
~ Catherine Pulsifer

"The smallest deed is better than the grandest intention."
~ Anonymous

Proverbs 21:21 ~ "Whoever pursues righteousness and kindness will find life and honor."

Galatians 5:22 ~ ". . . [T]he fruit of the Spirit is love, joy, peace, patience, kindness, generosity, faithfulness, . . ."

Prayer
Holy God,
As we see someone who needs help with simple tasks, give us the energy and desire to be the one who assists them with the task at hand. Help us remember that a simple helping hand could make the difference to them. Amen.

DAY 10 (31 overall): FAMILY

HAVE A MEAL WITH NO TELEVISION OR CELL PHONE— JUST TALK.

It's good to go "unplugged" during our meals. It gives us an opportunity to reconnect with family members with fewer distractions. My middle daughter has a basket next to the table for all cell phones during meals.

Here are some advantages of being unplugged:

1. You can actually enjoy the food you're eating.
2. Everyone can find out what other family members did during their day.
3. Parents get a sense of any issues facing another family member that need to be addressed.
4. You all get practice at talking with other people instead of texting.
5. Everyone can work on proper table manners, such as taking turns talking, saying "please" and "thank you," and not talking with your mouth full.

Don't let this time with your children pass you by because of unnecessary distractions. Unplug and get reacquainted. A friend said, "When you say yes to one thing, you are saying no to other things." Say yes to your family. It's important.

"When we work together, we have power to take problems
head on and make a huge difference in our life and
in the lives of others around us."
~ DAVID DENOTARIS

"Your cell phone has already replaced your camera, your calendar,
your alarm clock. . . . Don't let it replace your family."
~ @SNAPCONF

Isaiah 28:23 ~ "Listen, and hear my voice; Pay attention, and hear my speech."

I Timothy 4:16 ~ "Pay close attention to yourself and to your teaching; continue in these things, for in doing this you will save both yourself and your hearers."

Prayer

Listening God,

You have set an example for us to listen and make connections with others. Help us remember to follow that example with our family—to unplug and reconnect. Amen.

DAY 11 (32 overall): FAMILY

TEACH A CHILD TO BAKE BREAD OR OTHER BAKED GOODS.

I HAVE LOVED baking as long as I can remember. When I was 23, I was the baker for a private country club in Minnesota. Every year I made more rolls, blueberry muffins, and chocolate cake than most people bake in a lifetime. I enjoyed every minute of it. My grandmother and my mother both baked bread and rolls and taught me how.

Sharing your love of baking with a child can offer life-long benefits. One of the good things about baking is that the time between mixing up, baking, and eating is short. This maintains a child's attention span, and the delicious final product is its own reward.

But that's not all:

1. Measuring the ingredients helps with math skills (1/4 cup, 1/2 cup, etc.), especially if you double a recipe.
2. Maintaining cleanliness in the kitchen—both our personal hygiene and clean work surfaces—also presents a good lesson.
3. Knowing they're helping feed the family or making products to use for lunch boxes or in a meal is also a reward and builds self-esteem.
4. Baking encourages reading skills, from reading both the recipe and the labels of the ingredients.
5. Learning for young bakers includes scientific principles concerning leavening agents, heat applications, mixing versus over-mixing, and so on.

6. Baking encourages enthusiasm for making food at an early age, which can last and enhance a lifetime.
7. Decorating cakes, cupcakes, cookies, and the like encourages children to express their creative juices.
8. Baking is a way to help children develop fine motor skills with tasks such as measuring and mixing ingredients, cutting out cookies, cracking an egg, and kneading dough.

I have even baked virtually with my grown niece. We bake the same thing, visit while we work, and have a lot of fun.

My granddaughter Keagan, kneading dough

"What makes a difference in one person's life or in hundreds of lives is not merely a stack of checks; what makes a difference is you contributing your many gifts at your level and your capacity."
~ KATHY LEMAY, *THE GENEROSITY PLAN*

"Cooking with kids is not just about ingredients, recipes,
and cooking. It's about harnessing imagination,
empowerment, and creativity."
~ GUY FIERI

Leviticus 23:17 ~ "You shall bring from your settlements two loaves
of bread as an elevation offering, each made of two-tenths of an
ephah; they shall be of choice flour, baked with leaven, as first fruits
to the Lord."

Proverbs 22:6 ESV ~ "Train up a child in the way he should go;
even when he is old he will not depart from it."

Prayer
Father of everything good,
Thank You for helping us create with our hands the food we eat. We
are blessed to share that knowledge and creativity with others as
part of our legacy. Amen.

DAY 12 (33 overall): FAMILY

TELL SOMEONE IN YOUR FAMILY HOW MUCH THEY MEAN TO YOU.

THIS SOUNDS LIKE an easy, everyday thing to do, but how often
do we do it? We can take a lot of our family members for granted.
Or, our family situation may be less than desirable, and it could be
a difficult task.

You could be the person to change the interactions of your
entire family. Take this opportunity to tell one of them some of the
special things they have done for you. This can be scary or risky
because you don't know how they will respond, but think about
how much *you* would appreciate being told what you mean to
someone.

You could do one of the following:

1. Give them a simple gift with a handwritten card expressing some of their positive attributes.
2. Have a one-on-one dinner date to provide the opportunity to let them know how much they mean to you.
3. If they live far away, give them a call, write a text, or send a note.
4. Send a balloon bouquet with words on the balloons expressing their special attributes.
5. Send a copy of a family photo of a special time for both of you with a written note describing why you chose this photo and how important this time was in your life.

They have made a difference in your life; now you can make a difference in theirs.

Here's an example from Samantha Young of the kinds of things you might say to someone who means a lot to you:

"I laugh harder with you. I feel more myself with you. I trust you with me — the real me. When something goes wrong, or right, or I hear a funny joke, or I see something bizarre, you're the first person I want to talk to about it."[26]

"We won't always know whose lives we touched and made better for our having cared, because actions sometimes have unforeseen ramifications. What's important is that you do care, and you act."
~ CHARLOTTE LUNSFORD

Luke 15:11-32 ~ The Prodigal Son. I suggest you read the whole story. The son who left meant so much to his father that the father forgave him, took him back, and treated him like royalty. Such will our Heavenly Father do for us when we stray.

Ephesians 1:16 ~ "I do not cease to give thanks for you, remembering you in my prayers, . . ."

Prayer
Caring Jesus,
Thank You for making me feel important—important enough to die for me. Give me the courage to share with others what they mean to me and, in the process, make a difference in their lives. Amen.

DAY 13 (34 overall): FAMILY

HAVE A MEAL WITH YOUR FAMILY.

Eating together became a more frequent occurrence during the pandemic because people were encouraged to stay home. Before that, with everyone's busy schedules, it was difficult to find everyone home at dinner time. People had sports practices, games, other lessons, rehearsals, and dinner meetings, making it more difficult to be at the dinner table at the same time.

While eating together, you talk, reconnect, and spend time together. This maintains or grows relationships and gives everyone a sense of belonging. Isn't family the best place for that? Eating meals together also improves listening skills, which can transfer to the classroom and the workplace. You will also save money if you eat at home rather than going out, and you can make healthier choices at home because you know what ingredients are in every dish. It doesn't take that much time to prepare a meal, and if everyone helps, it increases your family bonding.[27]

"In essence, if we want to direct our lives, we must take control
of our consistent actions. It's not what we do once in a while that
shapes our lives, but what we do consistently."
~ Tony Robbins

"I think family mealtime is really important. There's a lot of
research that shows kids are going to do better in school and have
more self-esteem if you can all sit down and eat together."
~ Jewel

Deuteronomy 12:7 ~ "And you shall eat there in the presence of the Lord your God, you and your households together, rejoicing in all the undertakings in which the Lord your God has blessed you."

Acts 2:46 ~ "And day by day, attending the temple together and breaking bread in their homes, they received their food with glad and generous hearts...."

Prayer
Patient Lord,
As our family gathers at the dinner table, please bless our time together so it is a positive experience for all. Help us listen to each other and be respectful as we talk about our day. Amen.

DAY 14 (35 overall): FAMILY

RESOLVE A CONFLICT WITHIN YOUR FAMILY.

EVERY FAMILY WILL have disagreements and conflicts of some sort, big or small. Resolving them is the important thing. We need to do this not by burying them until they get bigger, but by using compromise, understanding, and peace before they turn into battles.

Bestselling author Karen Salmansohn suggests you use the following tactics to resolve family conflicts:[28]

1. **Get to the root of things.** You must get to the bottom of how it all began; talk about the core issues.
2. **Look at things from your family member's point of view.** Consider how you might have contributed in some way to the family fight. Find a way for everyone to apologize so feelings can be healed.
3. **Look at how this conflict affects the whole family.** What are the long-term repercussions of this family conflict? Who is caught up in this family dispute? Are you contributing

to the spread of anger to other family members? Again, examine your part in the conflict.

4. **Make the first move.** Sometimes if you want to move past a family rift, you need to be the "bigger" person and go beyond ego. Show you're willing to compromise and start the healing process. Swallow your pride and think about what the future holds for you both and the entire family.

5. **Talk it out on the phone.** You may feel less pressure chatting by phone than sitting face to face. Start out by asking how they are doing and talk to them warmly about their life. You need to strengthen the family bond before you launch into a difficult conversation.

If this approach doesn't resolve your conflict, get an unbiased third party involved. Life is too short to hold on to grudges, animosity, and disputes.

> "It takes ONE FAMILY to make a difference in this
> COMMUNITY. It takes ONE PERSON to make
> a difference in this FAMILY."
> ~ Nisandeh Neta

> "I learned that courage was not the absence of fear,
> but the triumph over it."
> ~ Nelson Mandela (1918-2013)

Romans 2:15 ~ "They show that what the law requires is written on their hearts, to which their own conscience also bears witness; and their conflicting thoughts will accuse or perhaps excuse them."

James 4:1 ~ "Those conflicts and disputes among you, where do they come from? Do they not come from your cravings that are at war within you?"

Prayer

Jesus, Healer of my soul,

Guide me to resolve any conflict that may have taken place within my family. Help me to be the first to step forward to address and solve any family issues. Amen.

Reflections from Week 5

1. The ways to make a difference I liked best this week were:

    ☐ Day 29   ☐ Day 32   ☐ Day 35
    ☐ Day 30   ☐ Day 33
    ☐ Day 31   ☐ Day 34

2. What did you do one on one? Where did you go and with whom?
3. Did a family member need help with their home or yard? What family member did you help and what did you do?
4. Is having a meal unplugged (no TV or cell phone) a common occurrence at your house? Was the family conversation better with no interruptions?
5. Whom did you teach and what did you bake? How was your time together?
6. Whom did you tell they mean a lot to you? What was their reaction? Did you tell more than one person?
7. Do you regularly have meals together as a family? Was this something new? How did you feel about eating and visiting with one another?
8. Was there a conflict within the family this week? Was it a new conflict or an ongoing one? How did you help resolve it?
9. Were you inspired to do something additional to the seven items for this week and, if so, what were they?
10. List some of the ways you felt while you were making a difference this week.

TEACH A CHILD A LIFE SKILL SUCH AS GARDENING, COOKING, SEWING.

AS A FORMER Home Economics teacher, it saddens me that Home Economics is not a regular part of the middle school curriculum. Life skills are called that for a reason. They are skills that, once learned, will help you for the rest of your life. Having these skills gives each of us confidence to meet the challenges of everyday life. Following are three of my own skills. What are yours?

1. **Gardening** is like working in a science lab. It nurtures curiosity. It can teach us about horticulture: how a seed grows into food or flower. It's a study of nature: looking at the seasons, the plants' needs, and what the plants do for us in return. It also teaches us about wildlife: the beneficial pollinators, the pests, and what we can do to nurture the beneficial and discourage the detrimental wildlife.

2. **Cooking** can improve our quality of life, save money, and improve our mental and physical health.

3. **Sewing** might simply involve learning to thread a needle and mending a tear or sewing on a button, or it might involve something more complicated such as making clothes.

    I learned to sew when I was eight years old. I started with easy projects and worked my way up to complicated garments, including my wedding dress. When I was in seventh grade Home Economics, we made a gathered skirt. Because I had mastered that skill years earlier, I made my gathered skirt along with a blouse that had set-in sleeves, cuffs, a collar, and buttonholes. Having these skills builds confidence. Start your child with a simple project like a pillow for a stuffed animal or doll, and move on to more detailed endeavors as they learn. If your own sewing skills are lacking, you can learn right along with your child.

You can pass many other life skills on to your children. Find skills they want to learn and go from there.

> "The greatest success we'll know is helping
> OTHERS succeed and grow."
> ~ Gregory Scott Reid

> "Teach me and I'll forget. Show me and I may remember.
> Involve me and I'll learn."
> ~ Benjamin Franklin (1706-1790)

Ecclesiastes 2:5 ~ "I made myself gardens and parks and planted in them all kinds of fruit trees."

Luke 5:36 ~ "He also told them a parable: 'No one tears a piece from a new garment and sews it on an old garment; otherwise, the new will be torn, and the piece from the new will not match the old.'"

Prayer

All-knowing God,
Encourage me to learn and teach life skills to make my life and the lives of others better. If I know something, help me share it. If I don't have the skill, help me learn it. Amen.

DAY 16 (37 overall): FAMILY

BE AN ADVOCATE FOR YOUR FAMILY MEMBERS.

Advocacy signifies the proactive support of a cause or an idea. It also involves arguing or pleading for a specific cause. Advocacy is practiced by an advocate, who may even plead the case in court. The main logic of advocacy is simply assisting people to communicate their views and be heard by the relevant people.

A family member might need an advocate in many stages of life:

1. A child may need an advocate in the classroom, in the doctor's office, with siblings, or with friends.
2. If you have a special needs child, you are their most important advocate because nobody knows your child as well as you do.
3. If a family member, spouse included, is in the hospital, they may not be capable of advocating for themselves, so you must do it for them.

    My daughter's husband had brain cancer and could not speak for himself, so she spoke strongly for him. She was the noisy wheel with the medical staff wherever he was. She knew what he needed and advocated on his behalf.
4. You may have elderly parents who can't communicate what they want or need. You can be their voice and advocate for them for care, benefits, financial help, and whatever's needed.

    When my mother could no longer speak, two of my sisters went to court to get guardianship to work with my brother who had Medical Power of Attorney, so they were Mom's advocates.

"You are not here merely to make a living. You are here in order to enable the world to live more amply, with greater vision, with a finer spirit of hope and achievement. You are here to enrich the world, and you impoverish yourself if you forget the errand."
~ WOODROW WILSON (1856-1924)

"Without advocacy vulnerable people cannot be heard or given credence. . . . They cannot be supported, protected or defended and their rights will be lost. Without advocacy vulnerable people have no power and will be invisible."
~ MICHELLE O'FLYNN

John 14:26 ~ "But the Advocate, the Holy Spirit, whom the Father will send in my name, will teach you everything, and remind you of all that I have said to you."

I John 2:1 ~ "My little children, I am writing these things to you so that you may not sin. But if anyone does sin, we have an advocate with the Father, Jesus Christ the righteous; . . ."

Prayer
Jesus the advocate,
Thank You for being my advocate every day. You talk to God on my behalf, pleading my case for forgiveness. Give me the courage to do the same for my family members. Amen.

DAY 17 (38 overall): FAMILY

BRING YOUR CHILDREN TO CHURCH.

WITH THE CURRENT state of the world, we need God in our lives more than ever. When children are babies, you can bring them where and when you want. Therefore, establish the habit when they are young, and they will become a part of a community of believers and will feel comfortable being there when they are older. If they've never been exposed to church, they will probably have a more difficult time making that a part of their everyday life.

Raising children in a church community is important in many ways. It provides a variety of role models of different ages, ethnicities, and backgrounds, which will enrich their lives and broaden their perspectives. The lessons taught in church will stay with them for life. They will remember the Ten Commandments, the importance of prayer, and the lessons taught in Bible stories. The relationships that are fostered there in a positive environment will help them in the good times and the not-so-good times.

"I want my child to have a strong faith in God because I know that faith will provide the comfort, solace, and inspiration to

carry him through the joys and tribulations that are
in store for him as a human."[29]
~ DEANNA MASCLE

"Making a profound difference in one specific child's life is
more powerful than describing the plight of
a million anonymous people."
~ DALE LOSCH, *A BETTER WAY*

Deuteronomy 11:19 ~ Regarding the Ten Commandments: "Teach
them to your children, talking about them when you are at home
and when you are away, when you lie down and when you rise."

3 John 1:4 ~ "I have no greater joy than to hear that my children
are walking in the truth."

Prayer
Protector of all,
Please help us train our children in the way You would want us to.
We know that Your way is the right way. Amen.

CHAPTER 3

MAKE A DIFFERENCE IN YOUR FRIENDS AND NEIGHBORS

THE RIPPLES ARE moving outward. They may be decreasing in size but are still important. As the first day of this new category, I want to share why you should do this so you'll want to hop on the ripples and make a difference.

Why Make a Difference in Your Friends and Neighbors?
Six good reasons are to:

1. show them you love them or care about them;
2. make the neighborhood a safer place to live, each one watching out for the others;
3. forge stronger bonds;
4. help in times of trouble as a family would (because so many of us have family far away);
5. let them know they can count on you;
6. help heal hurts.

DAY 1 (39 overall): FRIENDS AND NEIGHBORS

BE KIND.

Many years ago, I heard a phrase, came home, typed it up, and posted it on the refrigerator. It read, "There is never a good reason to be unkind."

Today's message is a good one for both kids and adults. It's to remind us that kindness matters, even in the smallest moments in our lives. Kindness has a positive impact on our brain and helps us live longer. Begin with being kind to yourself. Show self-worth and others will see your self-worth and treat you kindly. Not only that, but being kind becomes contagious and people pass on a small act of kindness to others, changing the people around us. It teaches us to see the best in others, making a difference in the world because we are all connected.[30]

"The smallest act of kindness is worth more
than the grandest intention."
~ Oscar Wilde (1854-1900)

"The Bottom Line on Kindness –
With research to back it up, it seems clear that doing good
for others can also do good for us. It's a habit that can be
developed anywhere, at any time, at little or no cost.
Actively work on this, make it a habit, and your
happiness quota will automatically skyrocket."[31]
~ Melody Pourmoradi

1 Peter 3:8 ESV ~ "Finally, all of you, have unity of mind, sympathy, brotherly love, a tender heart, and a humble mind."

Romans 15:2 ESV ~ "Let each of us please his neighbor for his good, to build him up."

Prayer
Kind and gentle Jesus,

Please guide my daily path to treat others as I want to be treated and be a constant example of kindness. Amen.

DAY 2 (40 overall): FRIENDS AND NEIGHBORS

STAND UP FOR SOMEONE BEING PICKED ON OR BULLIED.

YOU DON'T HAVE to be in school to see someone being picked on or bullied. Unfortunately, it can happen anywhere, to anyone. What do you do when you see someone being bullied?

In school, you could ask the bullied child how you can help, without judging them but showing them you care. You might ask if you can walk them home or if they want to join your group of friends. Being their friend goes a long way to their healing. A group of friends can band together, be brave, and face the bully as a group. If the bullying continues, confide in an adult you trust like a teacher, counselor, or the principal.

If it happens at the workplace, you should be a supportive friend there, too. Step in and separate the two, and try to understand why one is the bully and one is the victim. Help victims to stand up for themselves, either by themselves or along with you, and both of you make a plan. Most bullies look for someone vulnerable to pick on, so plan to catch the bully off guard and surprise them instead of them surprising you or your friend.[32] For example, Romans 12:20 says, ". . . if your enemies are hungry, feed them; if they are thirsty, give them something to drink; . . ." In other words, do something nice for them. This might get a bully on your side. If none of these things work, report the actions to Human Resources or someone else who can help.

By being a supportive friend, you can help the person being bullied, which will make a difference in their self-esteem and confidence, and give them courage to stand up for themselves.

"You are always stronger and more resourceful
than you give yourself credit for."
~ Rob Moore, START NOW, GET PERFECT LATER

"Sometimes the bravest and most important thing
you can do is just show up."
~ BRENÉ BROWN

Ephesians 6:14 ~ "Stand therefore, and fasten the belt of truth around your waist, and put on the breastplate of righteousness."

I Corinthians 16:13 ~ "Keep alert, stand firm in your faith, be courageous, be strong."

Prayer
God of the weak and vulnerable,
Please support my efforts to help my friends in difficult situations, showing Your love along the way. Help me encourage them and stick by them as friends should do. Amen.

HELP AN ELDERLY FRIEND/NEIGHBOR WITH GROCERY SHOPPING.

OUR ELDERLY POPULATION may need help with any number of things. Grocery shopping is one task that you can help with that makes a difference every day. You are probably going grocery shopping anyway, so just add a few of their needed items to your list and get the job done.

Or better yet, if they are able, take them with you. The outing, with physical activity and interaction with others, can be a great benefit to them. The elderly need the exercise; walking across the parking lot and through the store keeps their muscles working without overtaxing them. They will most likely see someone they know and stop for a little visit, which is also beneficial. Having you with them to shop the outer areas of the store where the fresh items are displayed can help their nutrition level as well. So, considering the social, physical, and nutritional benefits of a grocery store trip, it can make a difference in their ability to stay in their home longer and age successfully.

"Inspire, encourage, and uplift others—you may never realize the impact and influence you have made in another person's life."
~ ZIG ZIGLAR (1926-2012)

"If human beings are perceived as potentials rather than problems, as possessing strengths instead of weaknesses, as unlimited rather than dull and unresponsive, then they thrive and grow to their capabilities."
~ BARBARA BUSH (1925-2018)

Deuteronomy 28:50 ~ ". . . a grim-faced nation showing no respect to the old or favor to the young."

Proverbs 11:25 ~ "A generous person will be enriched, and one who gives water will get water."

Prayer
Lord of the old and the young,
Remind us that simple acts of kindness to people of all ages come right from Your example. Help us put ourselves in other peoples' shoes and acknowledge that they may need our help. Amen.

DAY 4 (42 overall): FRIENDS AND NEIGHBORS

BE ENTHUSIASTIC ABOUT A FRIEND'S OR NEIGHBOR'S PROJECT.

WHEN FRIENDS OR neighbors are working on a project, your enthusiasm can do a lot. This can be a project at home, on the job, or at school.

1. Your enthusiasm can increase their enthusiasm just at the point when they may need a boost in their momentum.
2. You may be more knowledgeable, so your enthusiasm may spur them on to ask you questions to make their end product better.
3. Your enthusiasm can motivate them to think outside the box.
4. You can reinforce their confidence, which encourages them if they're questioning their abilities and whether they should even be doing this project.
5. If they've finished the project, point out the positive aspects of it. Wait for them to ask you if they could improve it in any way before giving them your opinion.
6. If you are working on a project initiated by someone else, your enthusiasm can encourage their leadership so the project gets completed successfully.
7. If something goes awry on the project, your enthusiasm can help others regroup and reignite their enthusiasm.

Your enthusiasm can make a difference!

"Believe in yourself! Have faith in your abilities!
Without a humble but reasonable confidence in your
own powers you cannot be successful or happy."
~ Norman Vincent Peale (1898-1993)

"There is an eloquence in true enthusiasm."
~ Washington Irving (1783-1859)

1 Peter 5:2 ESV ~ "Shepherd the flock of God that is among you, exercising oversight, not under compulsion, but willingly, as God would have you; not for shameful gain, but eagerly; . . ."

Philippians 2:4 ESV ~ "Let each of you look not only to his own interests, but also to the interests of others."

Prayer

Jesus, creator of enthusiasm,

We are grateful for Your enthusiasm for our efforts. You may speak to us directly or encourage someone to show enthusiasm toward us. Either way, it spurs us on to do better and complete our projects. Help us to demonstrate that enthusiasm toward others. Amen.

Reflections from Week 6

1. The ways to make a difference I liked best this week were:

    ☐ Day 36   ☐ Day 39   ☐ Day 42
    ☐ Day 37   ☐ Day 40
    ☐ Day 38   ☐ Day 41

2. What life skill did you teach? Gardening, cooking, sewing, or another? To whom did you teach it? Will you do it again as an ongoing project?

3. Did you step out of your comfort zone and be an advocate for one of your family members? Who did you advocate for and how did you accomplish it?

4. Did you bring your children or grandchildren to church this week? Did you help them become comfortable being there? Will you do it again?

5. Did you go out of your way to be kind to your friends and neighbors? What did you do or say to them? How did they react?

6. Did you encounter anyone being bullied? What did you do? What was the result?

7. While you were grocery shopping, did you encounter someone who needed help? Did you help them? What was their reaction? How did that make you feel?

8. Did you find a friend or neighbor working on a project? What was the project? Were you enthusiastic and encouraging? What was the result?

9. Were you inspired to do something additional to the seven items for this week and, if so, what did you do?

10. List some of the ways you felt while you were making a difference this week.

DAY 5 (43 overall): FRIENDS AND NEIGHBORS

TAKE A FRIEND'S OR NEIGHBOR'S KIDS FOR THE DAY.

BEING A PARENT is not easy! Every now and then a break from your children is necessary and very welcomed. In some places, babysitting co-ops are available. I was a part of one for a while when my children were young. I also took my girls to daycare one day a week when they were young. That said, when someone else volunteered to take my kids for the day, it was a blessing. The amount of work I got accomplished during the time they were gone was remarkable. No interruptions made all the difference!

If you can offer that kind of respite to a friend or neighbor, I think they will be highly grateful. Then they can get some work done or just relax, take a bath, read something besides *Pat the Bunny,* or get caught up on sending letters or cards. Another bonus: It's good for children to interact with other adults and children.

"Do what you can, with what you have, where you are."
~ THEODORE ROOSEVELT (1859-1919)

"All of us, at some time or other, need help. Whether we're giving or receiving help, each one of us has something valuable to bring to this world. That's one of the things that connects us as neighbors—in our own way, each one of us is a giver and a receiver."
~ MR. (FRED) ROGERS (1928-2003)

Psalm 37:26 ~ "They are ever giving liberally and lending, and their children become a blessing."

I John 5:2 ~ "By this we know that we love the children of God, when we love God and obey his commandments."

Prayer
Jesus, lover of children,
Parenting can be a challenge. As much as we love our children,

sometimes we need a break from them to regroup and appreciate them more. Remind us to help other parents get a break from their children to make a difference in their lives. Amen.

DAY 6 (44 overall): FRIENDS AND NEIGHBORS

ENCOURAGE SOMEONE TO TRY SOMETHING NEW.

This is a wide-open topic. Something new—but *what* new thing? A new food, a new hairstyle, a new book genre, a new type of clothing, etc.? The list goes on. So many things could be new in our lives that this should be easy to accomplish. Be someone's cheerleader and encourage them to step out of their ruts, be adventurous, and try something new. (You, too!)

Once you've mastered the courage to try something new, you no longer have to be afraid of it and can be one step closer to who you want to be. It also exercises the creative part of your brain and gives you a new outlook on everything. Trying new things broadens your "body of work" and makes you more desirable as an employee and as a human.[33]

Encourage someone to explore new horizons. You could make a difference for them and put them on a new path.

My granddaughter cheering you on!

"When you learn something new, especially something that's not connected to your day job, it can be inspirational and life changing. Never stop learning, no matter how old you are, no matter what success you have achieved. It can be exciting and uplifting to learn a new skill!"
~ NORAH DEAY, *HOW TO BECOME THE GO-TO PERSON*

"Without experimentation, a willingness to ask questions and try new things, we shall surely become static, repetitive, and moribund."
~ ANTHONY BOURDAIN (1956-2014)

Isaiah 43:19 ~ "I am about to do a new thing; now it springs forth, do you not perceive it? I will make a way in the wilderness and rivers in the desert."

Isaiah 48:6 ~ "You have heard; now see all this; and will you not declare it? From this time forward I make you hear new things, hidden things that you have not known."

Prayer
God, Creator of all things,
Place the desire in our hearts to conquer our fears and be bold to experience for the first time what You have created. Give us courage to try new things, whether it is tasting a new food or branching out to try a new activity. Amen.

DAY 7 (45 overall): FRIENDS AND NEIGHBORS

LISTEN TO A FRIEND – JUST LET THEM TALK.

As a friend, sometimes we're called on to just listen. They don't want us to fix the problem, they just want to talk. To make your friend feel supported and valued, you need to not only listen but let them know you hear and understand what they're saying. Make sure the television and cell phones are turned off, because you don't want the conversation to get interrupted in the middle of a thought. Pay attention to them by looking directly at them and observing any clues they may be giving you such as tearing up or showing anger. Respond accordingly with a hand hold or a tissue. You don't have to give any verbal response, but use other ways to let them know you understand and support them. Then when the situation warrants it, ask a question or two. Mainly ask what they need from you—just someone to listen to them, a hug, or maybe some advice. Let them lead the conversation.[34]

Being there when they need you and being conscientious about listening and understanding are the best ways to show your friend that they can turn to you when they need someone who cares. If you're a good listener for them, they will probably be there for *you* when you need someone to listen.

"One of the most sincere forms of respect is
actually listening to what another has to say."
~ BRYANT H. McGILL

"You will heal and you will rebuild yourself around the loss you
have suffered. You will be whole again, but you will never be the
same. Nor should you be the same nor would you want to."
~ ELISABETH KUBLER-ROSS (1926-2004)

Proverbs 18:13 ESV ~ "If one gives an answer before he hears, it is
his folly...."

Proverbs 17:27 ~ "One who spares words is knowledgeable; one
who is cool in spirit has understanding."

Prayer
Dear Jesus, the great listener,
Teach us to be good listeners, be patient, and show compassion to
our friends who need a listening ear. Help us discern what they need
and be more of a listener than a speaker when the situation requires
it. Amen.

DAY 8 (46 overall) ~ FRIENDS AND NEIGHBORS

TELL OR SHOW SOMEONE YOU LOVE THEM.

MY SISTERS GIVE me credit for initiating hugs and telling family
members "I love you." This was years ago, and whether it's true or
not, I'm glad we hug and express our love.

To verbalize your affection to friends or neighbors can be
tricky. Gary Chapman wrote a book called *The Five Love Languages,* which outlines five general ways for partners to express
and experience love. Although he wrote it for partners, I believe it
would work for friends as well. He suggests acts of service, gift-giving, physical touch, quality time, and words of affirmation.[35] Fol-

lowing are my thoughts on those topics. I recommend Gary's book for many other suggestions.

1. **Acts of service** ~ Do something nice for a friend—something they need to get done and are unable to do themselves.
2. **Gift-giving** ~ Offer small tokens of caring, such as sharing some baked goods, bringing over dinner, sharing some garden produce, giving a gift on their birthday, or giving them something you know they need.
3. **Physical touch** ~ When they're sad, give a hug or a shoulder to cry on, or hold their hand in sympathy—or, give them a high-five or fist bump to congratulate them for something or celebrate something happy.
4. **Quality time** ~ Spend time with them by going out to lunch or dinner, going to a movie, playing golf, going to an art exhibit, or something else you both enjoy, or just having a cup of coffee together.
5. **Words of affirmation** ~ Encourage them, give them an "atta girl" or "atta boy," remind them of some of their positive attributes, or praise them for something they did well.

So even if you don't say the words "I love you"—although you can—the old saying "actions speak louder than words" can apply here. You never know what a difference you can make in your friend's or neighbor's life until you try.

"It is an absolute human certainty that no one can know his
own beauty or perceive a sense of his own worth until it
has been reflected back to him in the mirror of
another loving, caring human being."
~ John Joseph Powell (1893-1971), *The Secret of Staying in Love*

"Every gift from a friend is a wish for your happiness."
~ Richard Bach

John 3:16 ~ "For God so loved the world that he gave his only Son, so that everyone who believes in him may not perish but may have eternal life."

Galatians 5:14 ~ "For the whole law is summed up in a single commandment, 'You shall love your neighbor as yourself.'"

Prayer
Jesus, lover of my soul,
Encourage me to use the love languages you have demonstrated to me to show my friends and neighbors their worth to both You and me. Help me take the time to demonstrate Your love for them. Amen.

DAY 9 (47 overall): FRIENDS AND NEIGHBORS

TELL SOMEONE YOU'RE PROUD OF SOMETHING THEY'VE DONE OR WHO THEY ARE.

THERE'S NOTHING BETTER to hear from a friend than, "I'm proud of you for . . . !" That sentence gives the person speaking a chance to express their emotions, and it gives the recipient the good feeling that someone is proud of their accomplishments. It encourages them to keep up the good work. One of the best statements for me to hear is "I am proud to call you friend."

In this case, the word "proud" doesn't relate to Proverbs 16:18, "Pride goes before destruction, a haughty spirit before a fall." That statement is talking about an arrogant person who puts himself or herself above everyone else. Rather, saying you are proud of someone or praising them for something they've done well or who they are is meant to lift them up, to encourage them.

For example, you might praise others or tell them you're proud of them for . . .

1.   doing the right thing,
2.   achieving good grades in school,
3.   making good decisions,
4.   being promoted on the job,
5.   working hard,
6.   being a good parent, or
7.   being a good friend.

You might say something like, "You've always been the one to motivate me through the highs and lows, the good and bad, and you always seem to get yourself through tough times as well. I don't know how you always manage to pull yourself together, but you did it again. I'm proud of you."

If you feel uncomfortable saying your praise, you can always give your friend or neighbor a high-five or thumbs-up. Such actions as well as words make a difference.

"The best thing to give to your enemy is forgiveness; to an opponent, tolerance; to a friend, your heart; to your child, a good example; to a father, deference; to your mother, conduct that will make her proud of you; to yourself, respect; to all others, charity."
~ Benjamin Franklin (1706-1790)

"One of the most spiritual things you can do is embrace your humanity. Connect with those around you today. Say, 'I love you,' 'I'm sorry,' 'I appreciate you,' 'I'm proud of you' . . . whatever you're feeling. Send random texts, write a cute note, embrace your truth and share it . . . cause a smile today for someone else . . . and give plenty of hugs."
~ Steve Maraboli

Deuteronomy 26:19 ~ ". . . for him to set you high above all nations that he has made, in praise and in fame and in honor; and for you to be a people holy to the Lord your God, as he promised."

Matthew 12:18 ESV ~ "Behold, my servant whom I have chosen, my beloved with whom my soul is well pleased. I will put my Spirit upon him, . . ."

Prayer
Supportive God,
Help me demonstrate my pride in what others do by sincerely complimenting them on their accomplishments and encouraging them with my words or actions. Amen.

DAY 10 (48 overall): FRIENDS AND NEIGHBORS

TELL SOMEONE "YOU'VE GOT WHAT IT TAKES."

THE STRUGGLES OVER not feeling good enough are real. We're bombarded with so many things out there that it's not surprising we feel inadequate. We ask ourselves, "Am I a good enough spouse? Parent? Employee?" We want to be successful in whatever we choose to do, so telling someone they have what it takes to be successful is a deeply encouraging message.

Here are things you can do to help others reach their goals and reassure them they have what it takes:

1. Be supportive when they need to make changes.
2. Remind them to stay away from negative people who can bring them down.
3. Encourage them to keep moving forward when they face setbacks.
4. Help them *believe* they can succeed.

"Your belief determines your action, and your action determines your results, but first you have to believe."[36]
~ MARK VICTOR HANSEN

"Imagine what our real neighborhoods would be like if
each of us offered, as a matter of course,
just one kind word to another person."
~ Mr. (Fred) Rogers (1928-2003)

Judges 6:14 ~ "Then the Lord turned to him and said, 'Go in this might of yours and deliver Israel from the hand of Midian; I hereby commission you.'"

Isaiah 40:29 ~ "He gives power to the faint and strengthens the powerless."

Prayer
Thank You, Lord, for believing in me. You encourage me and put wonderful people in my life who also encourage me. Remind me to cheer others on to accomplish what You know they can do, and to support them in any way I can. Amen.

DAY 11 (49 overall): FRIENDS AND NEIGHBORS

INCLUDE SOMEONE IN AN ACTIVITY OR CLUB.

Whenever we move to a new neighborhood, we need to adjust. Meeting our new neighbors can be awkward.

Remember how it felt when *you* were the new person? Be welcoming to other new neighbors so they feel accepted.

After we moved to Midland, Michigan, my new neighbors gave me a baby shower because I was pregnant with our first baby. I met some of them for the first time at the shower. I felt very welcomed and accepted.

Invite new neighbors to come along on activities you have planned, such as a trip to a plant nursery, the library, or apple orchard, or a walk at a local garden. If you're a member of a church or club, invite them to come along to your church, garden club, card club, or herb group, for example. Or invite them to join you in a night out with friends. It doesn't take much to include someone, but it could make a big difference in their life.

Giving a presentation to my garden club, where we always welcome members' friends

"You have the power to make a difference in someone's life.
I continually hear personal stories of how one small
act of kindness warmed someone's soul."
~ ROBBIE MILLER KAPLAN, *HOW TO SAY IT WHEN YOU DON'T
KNOW WHAT TO SAY*

"There's always room in the heart for one more friend."
~ ANONYMOUS

James 2:1-4 ESV ~ "My brothers, show no partiality as you hold the faith in our Lord Jesus Christ, the Lord of glory. For if a man wearing a gold ring and fine clothing comes into your assembly, and a poor man in shabby clothing also comes in, and if you pay attention to the one who wears the fine clothing and say, 'You sit here in a good place,' while you say to the poor man, 'You stand over there,' or, 'Sit down at my feet,' have you not then made distinctions among yourselves and become judges with evil thoughts?"

Acts 17:4 ~ "Some of them were persuaded and joined Paul and Silas, as did a great many of the devout Greeks and not a few of the leading women."

Prayer
God of all friends,

Help me remember what it was like to be the new person in the neighborhood and treat others the way I wanted to be treated when I was new. Remind me to include them so they become familiar with their new surroundings. Amen.

Reflections from Week 7

1. The ways to make a difference I liked best this week were:

    ☐ Day 43   ☐ Day 46   ☐ Day 49
    ☐ Day 44   ☐ Day 47
    ☐ Day 45   ☐ Day 48

2. Did you help a friend or neighbor by taking their kids for the day? What did all of you do? Where did you go to pass the time? Were you tired at the end of the day?
3. How did you encourage someone to try something new? What was their response? If they were hesitant, how did you encourage them?
4. Did you have a friend who needed a listening ear? Did you just sit and listen? Was it easy or difficult for you to just listen? Did you help them solve their problem? How?
5. Who did you tell or show that you love them? What was their reaction?
6. How did you express your pride in another person's accomplishments? How did they respond?
7. Who did you tell that they have what it takes? How did you tell them and what was their reaction?
8. Did you invite someone to one of your club meetings? Who did you invite? Did they attend and, if so, how was their experience?
9. Were you inspired to do something additional to the seven items for this week and, if so, what did you do?
10. List some of the ways you felt while you were making a difference this week.

BRING A POT OF SOUP OVER TO A FRIEND OR NEIGHBOR IN NEED.

A GREAT WAY to help someone out is to bring them dinner. It doesn't need to be fancy; a pot of soup and some bread is always a good choice. A friend or neighbor in need could be someone who lost their job, had a death in the family or an accident, has a family member in the hospital, or is in any situation that puts a strain on the family. Not having to worry about dinner can be a real blessing under any circumstance but is even more appreciated in any of those circumstances. I have been the recipient and the giver many times, and I've been thankful for both the help and the opportunity to help.

Here's a great soup recipe that makes enough for you and to share:

Two kettles of soup using the following recipe

MINESTRONE SOUP
Ingredients:
1/2 cup dried haricot or soup beans OR a 16-ounce can baked beans
2-3 tablespoons olive oil
1-2 cloves garlic, crushed
1 medium onion, sliced

2 slices bacon cut in 1/2-inch pieces
4-5 cups brown or vegetable stock
1 stalk celery, finely sliced
1 leek, white only, cut into match-like shreds
2 small carrots, shredded
1/2 cup chopped cabbage
1-2 small zucchini, cut in strips
3/4 cup tomatoes, canned or fresh
6-7 green beans, chopped
2-3 tablespoons peas
3/4 cup macaroni
2 tablespoons chopped mixed parsley, basil, oregano, marjoram OR
1 tablespoon Italian Seasoning
GARNISH: 1 cup grated parmesan (or other hard cheese)

Directions:

Soak the soup beans overnight in cold water. Drain and put beans in a pan with 2 cups slightly salted water. Put the lid on the pan and bring to a boil. Simmer for 2 hours until tender. OR, use a 16-ounce can of baked beans.

In another pan, heat the oil and cook the garlic, onion, and diced bacon until golden brown. Add the beans, the stock, celery, leek, and carrots. Cook together for 20 minutes. Add finely sliced cabbage, zucchini, chopped tomatoes, green beans, peas, macaroni, and herbs. Cook for 15-20 minutes more. Season to taste and garnish with plenty of grated cheese in a separate bowl.

Give with love!

"What counts in life is not the mere fact that we have lived.
It is what difference we have made to the lives of others that
will determine the significance of the life we lead."
~ NELSON MANDELA (1918-2013)

"How much good inside a day?

Depends how good you live 'em.
How much love inside a friend?
Depends how much you give 'em."
~ Shel Silverstein (1930-1999)

II Chronicles 31:15 ~ "Eden, Miniamin, Jeshua, Shemaiah, Amariah, and Shecaniah were faithfully assisting him in the cities of the priests, to distribute the portions to their kindred, old and young alike, by divisions, . . ."

John 13:34-35 ESV ~ "A new commandment I give to you, that you love one another: Just as I have loved you, you also are to love one another. By this all people will know that you are my disciples, if you have love for one another."

Prayer

Living Savior,

You have put me in places where I can make a difference. Thank You. Let me be aware of others' needs and live my life in a way that pleases You and helps others. Amen.

DAY 13 (51 overall): FRIENDS AND NEIGHBORS

ASK ANOTHER PERSON FOR HELP.

To ASK SOMEONE else for help can be a humbling experience. You may think it shows weakness and vulnerability because you're risking rejection, criticism, or feeling exposed, and you would rather do it yourself than subject yourself to that. Sometimes, however, the circumstances require you to ask for help. So instead of simply considering your own feelings, consider those of the person from whom you're asking help. You'll see that asking them for help will make them feel important and valued.

When you ask them, use language that shows your recognition of their unique abilities. By including someone else, you're making your workload and responsibilities lighter. Not only that, but you're developing a more meaningful relationship with that person, reaching outside your comfort zone, and finding individuals you can count on to support you.

Remember how it feels when you help someone else. Helping people makes everyone feel good—the person helping as well as the person needing help. We are not superheroes; we can't do everything alone. Make someone feel important. Ask for their help and make a difference in both your lives.

"Someone else will help. If we all thought that way no help would be given to anyone. We are all busy, we all have many demands on our time. We all can spare an hour. How many hours do we waste in a run of a month? If you just took one of those wasted hours and gave it to help others, you would be making a positive difference in the lives of others."
~ Catherine Pulsifer, *You Can Certainly Help*

"Don't be afraid to ask questions. Don't be afraid to ask for help when you need it. I do that every day. Asking for help isn't a sign of weakness, it's a sign of strength. It shows you have the courage to admit when you don't know something, and to learn something new."
~ Barack Obama

Philippians 4:6-7 ~ "Do not be anxious about anything, but in everything by prayer and supplication with thanksgiving let your requests be made known to God. And the peace of God, which surpasses all understanding, will guard your hearts and your minds in Christ Jesus."

Matthew 8:5 ~ "When Jesus had entered Capernaum, a centurion came to him, asking for help."

Prayer

Helping Jesus,

Sometimes the burden of doing everything myself weighs heavily on me. I know You work through all of us. Remind me to ask others for help to lighten my load and help them feel valued, knowing it's good for both of us. Amen.

DAY 14 (52 overall): FRIENDS AND NEIGHBORS

CHECK ON YOUR ELDERLY NEIGHBORS.

MANY OF US don't have family living close by. We can be surrogate children and check on elderly friends. I am sure they would appreciate some visitors, especially if they're living alone. Bring them something to eat, a game to play, or just a listening ear. See if they have any needs and make sure they're healthy and safe.

Loneliness is a real problem for the elderly. When I was about seven years old, our next-door neighbor was elderly and living alone. As a child, I would go over and visit with Mrs. Peterson. She would always give me a snack and some paper and crayons to draw her a picture.

Your neighbor would appreciate the company, and the history they could share would be priceless.

They may need help with . . .

1. a minor repair,
2. getting to a doctor,
3. winterizing their home,
4. turning on their furnace in cold weather,
5. catching up on local news,
6. dispersing of medications, or
7. going through mail and paying bills.

And the list goes on, so just ask.

You could be a life saver, making a difference for your elderly neighbor.

A minister told this story to his congregation one Sunday morning:

A few days ago, a Kentucky garbage man noticed no trash cans were being put out at an elderly woman's house on his route for two straight weeks. He was concerned enough to share the address with his supervisor. She found the name of the woman at the address and called her:

"Ms. Smith, we noticed you haven't put out your cans for a while. Are you ok?"

Ms. Smith replied: "I'm ok. But my caretaker was so afraid of the virus that she stopped coming. I can't get to the store. I don't have any trash because I've run out of food. And I don't have any family to help me."

After a long pause, the caller said: "You do now. We are your family."

She let her truck driver know of the sad news.

The next day, on his day off, he knocked on her door and asked her to make up a grocery list. "Ms. Smith—the list is too short." She added a few more items. "Ms. Smith, this list is still too short. Would you mind if I looked into your fridge?" She relented. He opened the fridge, and it was bare. Empty.

An hour later, he brought in dozens of bags of groceries for a woman he hardly knew. Tears. An air-hug that met social distancing protocol. And the garbage man walked out of the house of this woman who was physically immobile but levitating.

The garbage man decided he'd reach out to someone. The church broke out. His supervisor shared the creed with this elderly woman: ["You have a family now."]

The elderly lady said, "I miss our services of worship. I miss that it's silent now. I'm sick to my stomach we had to push back our start-back date to gather."

But church? Church is happening all around us. It's a phone call. It's a bag of groceries. It happens anytime

someone tells another person who is Jesus in His best disguise: ["You have a family now."] Real church is not defined by a service of worship, but by servants of Christ. Keep being church. That's all you have to do.
~ Author unknown

"It is one of the most beautiful compensations of life that no man can sincerely try to help another without helping himself."
~ Ralph Waldo Emerson (1803-1882)

"We have this day and the rest of our lives, however long that may be, to make a difference, change our behavior, take action, and do the things we've always dreamed of."
~ Scott Allan, *Do It Scared*

Psalm 71:9 ~ "Do not cast me off in the time of old age; do not forsake me when my strength is spent."

Matthew 9:36 ~ "When he saw the crowds, he had compassion on them, because they were harassed and helpless, like sheep without a shepherd."

Prayer
Caring God,
As we go through our days, help us remember to be observant and identify someone who may need help, especially our elderly neighbors. Maybe we should write it on our calendar to do a regular check on them and "Be their family now." Amen.

DAY 15 (53 overall): FRIENDS AND NEIGHBORS

GO FOR A WALK WITH A FRIEND.

Day 17's suggestion was GO ON A NATURE WALK—for yourself. Today, share your walk with a friend. Just walking is good exercise, but walking with a friend makes the time pass more quickly and provides a connection with someone else—and you still get the benefit of being outside. You can enjoy God's beauty and have great conversations along the way. Depending on where you live, you can observe the variety in the seasons—the changing leaves on the trees, perhaps a V of geese squawking high above you, a bird making a nest in the spring, a beautiful garden, or the humorous antics of a couple of squirrels.

Many years ago, a friend and I planned to walk in the mornings. When one of us wasn't up for it, the other encouraged us to keep our date, so not wanting to let the other one down, we walked. Having another person along helps you keep motivated during the walk, so you may walk farther than originally planned. Walking with someone else makes memories the two of you share. If each of you has fitness goals for yourself, the other person can help you stick to your plan to reach your goals.

Walking with someone else stimulates interesting and educational discussions, provides helpful hints to solve problems, and forms a strong bond between the two of you. Plus, it's more fun with another person. Walking together provides a chance to have one-on-one time without all the usual interruptions. You each can make a difference in the other's life.

The idea of walking with another also raises helpful analogies about life:

"Walking a mile in someone else's shoes isn't as much about the walk or the shoes; it's to be able to think like they think, feel what they feel, and understand why they are who and where they are. Every step is about empathy."
~ TONI SORENSON

"If you want to walk fast, walk alone, but if you want to walk far, walk together."
~ UNKNOWN ORIGIN

Proverbs 10:9 ~ "Whoever walks in integrity walks securely, but whoever follows perverse ways will be found out."

Acts 3:6-8 ~ "But Peter said, 'I do not possess silver and gold, but what I do have I give to you: In the name of Jesus Christ the Nazarene—walk!' And seizing him by the right hand, he raised him up; and immediately his feet and his ankles were strengthened. With a leap he stood upright and began to walk; and he entered the temple with them, walking and leaping and praising God."

Prayer
Oh Lord Jesus,
We ask that You give us the incentive to walk, and better yet, walk with a friend. Help us make a lasting connection with the person we walk with as well as get the exercise we could use. Amen.

HELP A NEW NEIGHBOR GET ACQUAINTED WITH YOUR COMMUNITY.

WHEN I FIRST moved to Midland, Michigan, our next-door neighbor brought me to the Farmers' Market. He told me to walk around the entire market, see what's available, then choose the items to purchase on the second go round. I still do it that way because it was good advice.

Show your new neighbor some of your favorite places—restaurants, the library, museums, parks, and so on. Most important, remember the things your neighbors did for you when you were new.

Our first experience when the moving van was unloading was, "Hi. I live next door. When I saw your canoe on the front lawn, I knew you were good people." What a wonderful greeting—but you could just say hello or wave.

You could also offer help as they're moving in. If their children are young and slowing down their progress, offer to take the kids and play with them for an hour or so, or help carry in some boxes. If it's summertime, you could have a block party potluck for everyone to meet and give cards with information about your families and the neighborhood. If you want to do something simpler, just bring over a plate of cookies or a welcome basket with some of your favorite things. Our neighbor let us use his lawnmower because we didn't have one and couldn't afford to buy one right away.

Stay connected with your new neighbors by checking in periodically. Help them feel at home in the neighborhood. Such a welcome could really make a difference.

"If you want happiness for an hour – take a nap.
If you want happiness for a day – go fishing.
If you want happiness for a month – get married.
If you want happiness for a year – inherit a fortune.
If you want happiness for a lifetime – help others."
~ CHINESE PROVERB

"Our American tradition of neighbor helping neighbor has always been one of our greatest strengths and most noble traditions."
~ RONALD REAGAN (1911-2004)

Mark 10:45 ~ "For even the Son of Man did not come to be served, but to serve, and to give his life as a ransom for many."

James 1:22 ~ "But be doers of the word and not merely hearers who deceive themselves."

Prayer
Welcoming Lord,
Thank You for putting other people in our lives. Help us remember what it felt like to be the new person in the neighborhood and to do our best at making others feel welcomed. Amen.

HELP YOUR NEIGHBOR IN AN EMERGENCY.

Of course, we hope no one in our group of friends or neighbors has an emergency situation, but chances are someone will. An emergency can affect a large area, like a flood or wildfire. In those cases, often neighbors help neighbors; they are all in the same situation and understand what the others are feeling.

Before an emergency arises, you can find out the following information ahead of time so you'll be prepared:

1. How many people live in the house?
2. What are their ages?
3. Do any of them have chronic medical conditions?
4. Are any of the residents vulnerable, e.g., single parent, disabled, elderly?
5. What skills do the members of your neighborhood have? Are any of them medical personnel, such as a doctor or nurse? Is anyone a plumber, electrician, firefighter, or policeperson?
6. Get their phone numbers and give them yours, and let them know they can count on you for help.

Be prepared to help those in need with food, first aid supplies, medicines, clean water, hygienic supplies, and warm clothes as needed and available. Should a disaster strike, check on your neighbors, especially the vulnerable ones, and offer help. If you have electricity and they don't, ask if you can notify their relatives or let them use your phone to get the help they need or use your power to charge their own phones. They may need refrigerator or freezer space for some of their food, so be ready and willing to share yours as you can.

Sometimes an emergency affects one neighbor and requires a rapid response. You could drive them to the hospital or call an ambulance, potentially saving a life. This could make a critical difference that would make them forever grateful.

"We all have dreams. . . . We all want to believe deep down
in our souls that we have a special gift, that we can make a
difference, that we can touch others in a special way,
and that we can make the world a better place."
~ TONY ROBBINS, *Awaken the Giant Within*

"The two most important days in your life are the day you
are born and the day you find out why."
~ ANONYMOUS

I Corinthians 10:24 ~ "Do not seek your own advantage, but that of the other."

Philippians 2:3 ~ "Do nothing out of selfish ambition or vain conceit. Rather, in humility value others above yourselves, . . ."

Prayer
Dearest Savior,
Encourage us to be familiar with our neighbors so we can help them if disaster hits. We want to do Your work with our hands when people need help. Make us aware and available to do just that. Amen.

DAY 18 (56 overall): FRIENDS AND NEIGHBORS

VISIT A FRIEND IN THE HOSPITAL.

MOST OF US have been in the hospital as a patient at some point in our lives and know how wonderful it is to have visitors, depending on the circumstances. Generally, visits from family and friends reduce a patient's anxiety and stress, which helps speed up the healing.

That said, before you go, call ahead and see if it's a good time to visit. I remember when I was in the hospital after lung surgery. A friend called and asked if she could visit. The physician's assistant had just removed tubes from my lungs with no pain killer, and I was in rough shape. I was glad my friend called first, because I was not yet ready for visitors. I felt bad afterwards, but our visit would not have been very pleasant given I was in so much pain.

When you call, ask if you can bring something they might need or like, such as a food treat (if allowed) or a book or magazine. For example, when my husband was in the hospital, I brought him three Sudoku puzzle books to help him pass the time.

Be sure you don't stay too long. People in the hospital need to sleep to heal. When I was in the hospital after the birth of my third child, the young mother across the hall from me had visitors all day long. (I felt I should go over and serve sandwiches to all of them!) I overheard her say several times, "I'm tired," when asked how she was. No one ever got the hint. Let the patient rest and eat so their stay isn't prolonged.

Here are some Dos and Don'ts for hospital visits:

Do . . .

1. ask the patient for permission to visit;
2. ask about hospital protocols: Are masks required? What are visiting hours?
3. wash your hands and/or sanitize them;
4. consider allergies and restrictions on decorations and gifts;
5. turn off cell phones;
6. keep your visit short;
7. leave if the doctor or provider arrives.

Don't . . .

1. visit if you might be contagious;
2. bring young children;
3. bring food without checking on restrictions;
4. cause stress for the patient;

5. avoid visiting, unless there's a practical or medical reason you shouldn't;
6. smoke before or during your visit.

When you have permission, a visit from you could make a difference to both the patient and you. When my dad was in the hospital in his last hours, two of my sisters and I sang hymns to him in his room with the door open. A nurse came in, and I thought she was going to tell us to stop. Instead, she told us what a blessing we were to the other patients.

> ". . . [E]ach time we make a difference in someone else's life,
> no matter how small, it will encourage them to do the
> same for others. And each time that happens,
> we all become a stronger force for good."
> ~ THOMAS E. PIERCE, *THE LAST ROSE*

> "The greatest healing therapy is friendship and love."
> ~ HUBERT HUMPHREY (1911-1978)

Zechariah 7:9 ~ "This is what the LORD Almighty said: 'Administer true justice; show mercy and compassion to one another.'"

Matthew 11:28 ~ "Come to me, all you who are weary and burdened, and I will give you rest."

Prayer
Heavenly healer,
When someone close to us is in the hospital, help us be respectful with our visits so our visit will be healing, not a hassle. Help us do what is best for them. Amen.

Reflections from Week 8

1. The ways to make a difference I liked best this week were:

    ☐ Day 50   ☐ Day 53   ☐ Day 56
    ☐ Day 51   ☐ Day 54
    ☐ Day 52   ☐ Day 55

2. Did you have a neighbor or friend in need this week? Did you bring them a meal? What was their reaction? Will you do it again?
3. Did you ask someone for help? Have you ever asked for help before? What was their reaction?
4. Do you have any elderly friends or neighbors? Did you check on them with a visit? Did you bring something to give them? What did you find there?
5. Did you encourage a friend to go for a walk with you? What was their reaction? How did you both feel after the walk?
6. Do you have a new family in your neighborhood? How did you help them feel welcome?
7. Was there an emergency in your neighborhood? How did you help?
8. Did you have a friend in the hospital? Did you visit them? Did you bring them something, and if so, what was it?
9. Were you inspired to do something additional to the seven items for this week and, if so, what did you do?
10. List some of the ways you felt while you were making a difference this week.

DAY 19 (57 overall): FRIENDS AND NEIGHBORS

OFFER TO WATER A FRIEND'S PLANTS AND CHECK ON THEIR HOUSE WHILE THEY'RE AWAY.

IF YOU'RE A gardener, you know how important flowers, vegetables, and herbs are to a fellow gardener. It may not seem like much, but keeping a friend's or neighbor's plants watered while they're on vacation is particularly important to the person growing them. They have nurtured the plants for several months or years and to have them die while they're on vacation for lack of water would be discouraging if not disastrous.

Before your friend leaves, make sure they check for any pests. You have your own yard to take care of and to treat the plants for insect damage is asking a little more than you probably have time to do. If it's winter, the indoor plants require watering, too.

Also, have your friend check to make sure everything is running as it should: the furnace, water heater, and freezer (and make sure the door is closed tight). Have them make sure the toilet *isn't* running continually, etc. before they leave. Then check while they're away to make sure everything is still running properly. We all have heard stories of water damage inside the house while people are away. They'll be happy you were watching out for them. You can make a difference both inside and out!

"As far as service goes, it can take the form of a million things. To do service, you don't have to be a doctor working in the slums for free or become a social worker. Your position in life and what you do doesn't matter as much as how you do what you do."
~ ELISABETH KUBLER-ROSS (1926-2004) QUOTED IN *TEACHERS IN WISDOM*, 2010

"Definition of good neighbor: someone to be trusted; a courteous, friendly source of help when help is needed; someone you can count on; someone who cares."
~ EDWARD B. RUST

Ephesians 5:1 ~ "Follow God's example, therefore, as dearly loved children."

I Peter 3:8 ~ "Finally, all of you, be like-minded, be sympathetic, love one another, be compassionate and humble."

Prayer
Helper God,
As we reflect on the times others have helped us while we traveled, encourage us to reciprocate while they travel. We don't want them to come home to a disaster after a relaxing vacation and find things out of order. Help us be good friends and neighbors. Amen.

DAY 20 (58 overall): FRIENDS AND NEIGHBORS

COOK WITH A FRIEND AND SHARE THE FINISHED PRODUCTS.

I HAVE ENJOYED cooking for a long, long time! The creative aspect drew me in. Many times, I have cooked with others, whether I was preparing with others for a class I was teaching or practicing dishes we learned when taking a class. I have cooked with my sister-in-law for fun and when preparing food for a party. Cooking with others can be very enjoyable—and eating what you made together extends the enjoyment.

Cooking can also be therapeutic! It helps mental health because you use your creative side. It channels your energy and distracts from the worries of the day.

When you begin to cook, if you aren't experienced, start with a beginner's cookbook. If the person you're cooking with is more experienced than you are, you can learn new skills. It's a great way to connect with others and make life more enjoyable while spending quality time together.

After teaching Home Economics for several years, I noticed the students were always glad for the reward at the end of class— eating what they cooked. They learned about nutrition and making good food choices, and found that cooking with and for others is a reward in itself. And besides all that, they had fun!

Enjoying one another's company and being creative at the same time can make a positive difference to all who participate.

My friend Irene and I making pasta in Italy

"The more we care for the happiness of others,
the greater our own sense of well-being becomes."
~ THE DALAI LAMA

"You can't use up creativity. The more you use,
the more you have."
~ MAYA ANGELOU (1928-2014)

Ecclesiastes 9:7 ESV ~ "Go, eat your bread with joy, and drink your wine with a merry heart, for God has already approved what you do."

Acts 2:46 ESV ~ "And day by day, attending the temple together and breaking bread in their homes, they received their food with glad and generous hearts, praising God and having favor with all the people."

Prayer
Most Holy God,
We thank You for our friends. We are blessed by them every day. Thank You for supplying all we need to be creative and prepare food for ourselves and others. Help us make the food taste good and nourish our bodies. Amen.

CHAPTER 4

MAKE A DIFFERENCE IN YOUR COMMUNITY

IN THIS CATEGORY the ripples move out slightly from your neighborhood to your community. There are things happening in your community that aren't necessarily happening with your friends and neighbors. Jump in to help and make a difference!

Why Make a Difference in Your Community?
Six good reasons are to:

1. be a good steward of where you live;
2. help the less fortunate or those in trouble;
3. make your community a prettier place to live;
4. help local businesses thrive;
5. move outward and help children make a difference;
6. show understanding to others.

> "An act of kindness to a neighbor
> is a blessing to the entire community."
> ~ ELIZABETH THATCHER, *WHEN CALLS THE HEART*,
> HALLMARK CHANNEL

DAY 1 (59 overall): YOUR COMMUNITY

HANDWRITE A THANK YOU NOTE.

HANDWRITING A THANK you note can seem like a lost art with all our electronic communication. These days it's more likely a "thx" in a text. To me, it's much more meaningful to write your thoughts down and "snail mail" a card to someone. Receiving something in the mail that's not an advertisement is heartwarming and indicates the sender's sincerity, especially if it's a heartfelt, handwritten note. Hallmark's motto is "When you care enough to send the very best." You took the time to pick out the card, write a note, put a stamp on it, and mail it; that says you care and makes your relationship with the receiver stronger. Everyone likes to know people appreciate their gifts, whether the gifts are of time and effort or a physical nature.[37]

You can write a thank you note to someone who sent you a gift, did something nice for you, went out of their way to make you feel special, helped someone in your family, or anything for which you're grateful. Remember, it takes you only a few minutes to write, and it's worth every minute. Not only does it show you're thankful, but it sends a message to others to show *their* gratitude when people go out of their way to do something nice.

Acts of kindness, either on the job or in your personal life, always need to be acknowledged. Whether thanking someone for their time in a job interview, watching your kids for an afternoon, or helping you with a project, a card reinforces their behavior and kindness. It indicates their action was meaningful to you and makes them feel good.

Despite the ease of electronic communication—or maybe in defiance of it—handwritten thank you notes are coming back in popularity. If you're feeling thankful, let someone know by taking the time and effort to write them a note. When was the last time you received or sent a thank you note? Didn't both receiving and sending one make you feel good? Write one and make a difference in someone's life.

"Today, many will take the action necessary to
make a difference. Why not you?"
~ STEVE MARABOLI, *WHY NOT YOU*

"A little Consideration, a little Thought for Others,
makes all the difference."
A. A. MILNE AS EEYORE IN *WINNIE-THE-POOH*

Romans 12:2 ~ "Do not be conformed to this world, but be transformed by the renewing of your minds, so that you may discern what is the will of God—what is good and acceptable and perfect."

1 Timothy 4:4-5 ESV ~ "For everything created by God is good, and nothing is to be rejected if it is received with thanksgiving, for it is made holy by the word of God and prayer."

Prayer
Good and gracious God,
You overwhelm us with Your generosity. Remind us to thank You for all the gifts You have given us. Help us to be thankful for our friends and to our friends for their thoughtful gestures and write them a thank you note telling them so. Amen.

DAY 2 (60 overall): YOUR COMMUNITY

SHARE SOME GARDEN FLOWERS WITH RETIREMENT HOME RESIDENTS.

IF YOU ARE a gardener and have some garden flowers growing, why not cut a bouquet and share it with a nursing home resident? The cheerful flowers will let them know someone cares and may lift their spirits.

Some years ago, our church women's group bought potted flowers in the spring for each resident in a local retirement home. It made them all happy. They now had something to care for besides themselves. The flowers looked pretty and added beauty to each of their apartments.

Flowers in a residence may . . .

1. reduce stress,
2. boost the resident's mood,
3. lift the spirits of both men and women,
4. bolster relationships,
5. boost the resident's memory,
6. help the resident sleep better—especially lavender, and
7. help the resident heal physically.[38]

A little gesture of kindness goes a long way to make a difference in another's life.

Flowers from my garden

"I also believe in the wisdom of the saying 'What goes around comes around.' When you help others, it does come back to you. And it does not have to be a big thing, even a small token of help can make a huge difference in the lives of someone else. So, the

next time you are feeling down or overwhelmed with your own issues, help someone else. It will bring much happiness into your own life. And you will have made a difference in the life of someone else. And is that not a purpose of each of our lives— to make a difference to other people?"
~ CATHERINE PULSIFER, *CHEER AN INSPIRATIONAL THOUGHT*[39]

"Flowers always make people better, happier and more helpful; they are sunshine, food and medicine for the soul."
~ LUTHER BURBANK

Luke 12:27 ESV ~ "Consider the lilies, how they grow: they neither toil nor spin, yet I tell you, even Solomon in all his glory was not arrayed like one of these."

Isaiah 32:8 ~ "But those who are noble plan noble things, and by noble things they stand."

Prayer
Thoughtful God,
Help us think of what we can do for others as You would have us do. Remind us how a simple act of thoughtfulness, like sharing flowers, can lift someone's spirits and brighten their day. Encourage us to take the time to be kind. Amen.

DAY 3 (61 overall): YOUR COMMUNITY

SEND A GET-WELL CARD OR EXPRESS WELL WISHES.

MOST OF US are familiar with Alex Trebek from *Jeopardy,* the television game show. After he announced he was diagnosed with stage 4 pancreatic cancer, he received hundreds of thousands of well wishes. A while later, Trebek reported that his cancer was in "near remission," saying his doctors "hadn't seen this kind of positive results in their memory."[40]

Wow! You never know what beneficial impact heartfelt cards and well wishes can have.

Richard Gunderman, the Chancellor's Professor, Schools of Medicine, Liberal Arts, and Philanthropy, Indiana University, Indianapolis, Indiana, notes: "The most immediately apparent benefits of well wishes accrue to recipients. When we are injured, sick or suffering, knowing that someone else is thinking about us can be a source of comfort. It counteracts one of the worst aspects of suffering – isolation."[41]

Gunderman continues: "The recent outpouring of well wishes for a television game show host—a stranger to most who reached out to him – offers an important insight into what makes families, friendships and communities thrive. Connectedness and its benefits are not something we should take for granted. Whether in the form of a simple text message or greeting card – or better yet, a phone call or a visit – letting someone who is hurting know that we care can make a big difference for all."[42]

For those of us *giving* the well wishes, thinking of others and building connections make us happier and make the world a better place to live.

> "When God puts love and compassion in your heart
> toward someone, He's offering you an opportunity
> to make a difference in that person's life."
> ~ Joel Osteen

> " . . . [T]here are plenty of warm, hopeful, encouraging and even
> funny things you can say to someone who's injured or ill. And
> whatever you write, the simple gesture of reaching out with a card
> will go a long way toward lifting that person's spirits."
> ~ Keeley Chase, Hallmark

Proverbs 21:2 ~ "All deeds are right in the sight of the doer, but the Lord weighs the heart."

Galatians 6:9 ~ "So let us not grow weary in doing what is right, for we will reap at harvest time, if we do not give up."

Prayer
Living God,
As we think of others' needs, particularly those suffering from ill health, remind us to contact them, expressing our thoughts and prayers for them to get well, remembering how we felt receiving a card or well wishes in similar circumstances. Amen.

DAY 4 (62 overall): YOUR COMMUNITY

PAY IT FORWARD.

THE FIRST-YEAR ANNIVERSARY of when my son-in-law passed away from brain cancer, my 35-year-old daughter and their two young children, ages four and six, went to two of his favorite restaurants and bought food for other patrons to "pay it forward." It was a good lesson for their kids, and it made my daughter feel good to honor him in that way. They have made it a tradition and have continued to do similar things since then.

This random act of kindness as well as paying for the person's order behind you in line at the drive-thru has become quite popular. Doing this brightens the day of the person who got a free order, and it makes you feel good, surprising someone. The news media wrote up the story when 167 cars in a row paid it forward to the car behind them at a fast-food chain![43]

Giving makes us happier. As social beings, the joy of giving creates happiness in the brain, which makes us healthier. Stress levels drop when joy levels rise. Lower stress levels boost our immune system, which gives us the ability to fight off diseases.

Kindness builds communities. A Michigan University study found that college students in the 1970s had 40 percent more empathy than young people they interviewed in 2010 on campus. They attributed this drop to the fact we've become less trusting and less giving.[44] Showing neighborly kindness can reduce many of the social ills plaguing communities and break down the barriers that prevent us from helping one another.

We must be more tolerant and understanding of each person, no matter what their race, color, or creed, for they face the same struggles we do. We all may need a helping hand now and then, so let's pay close attention to the signs others are giving us and provide help when possible.

> "It's the simple, unexpected acts of generosity that
> can change lives, and a culmination of these
> small acts can change the world."[45]
> ~ Whitney Anthony

> "It is life's principle, and you have to accept it as it comes;
> nothing happens when nothing is done."
> ~ Israelmore Ayivor, *Let's Go to the Next Level*

Psalm 100:5 ~ "For the LORD is good; his steadfast love endures forever, and his faithfulness to all generations."

Acts 20:35 ESV ~ "In all things I have shown you that by working hard in this way we must help the weak and remember the words of the Lord Jesus, how he himself said, 'It is more blessed to give than to receive.'"

Prayer
Almighty God,
Your Son, Jesus, paid for our salvation by dying on the cross. In gratefulness, let us be an example and pay it forward to help others from every walk of life. Small things add up and we could make a big difference by doing small things for others. Amen.

BE A MENTOR.

BEING A MENTOR is beneficial for the child or adult you are mentoring and for you.

Mentees . . .

1. learn something they didn't know or get help with something they had trouble doing or understanding;
2. may become the next generation of leaders;
3. increase their confidence (particularly women in male-dominated fields);
4. have a better sense of well-being knowing the mentor is on their side;
5. get exposed to fresh perspectives, ideas, and approaches;
6. have increased success, satisfaction, career and promotion opportunities.

Mentors . . .

1. see their positive influence on the one they're mentoring;
2. experience growth in their own field from answering the mentee's questions;
3. experience the spiritual rewards of donating their skill and time to help others;
4. have the satisfaction of nurturing success and providing knowledge and advice to allow the mentee a way to overcome challenges;
5. build a life-long bond with the mentee;
6. experience the great feeling of making a difference.

"By becoming a mentor, you will touch the life of a child,
make a difference for tomorrow's youth, and give back to your
community by investing in a young person who will,
in turn, mentor the next generation."
~ THOMAS DORTCH, *THE MIRACLES OF MENTORING*

"Why not go out on a limb? That's where the fruit is."
~ Written by journalist Frank Scully in 1950

1 Peter 5:2-4 ESV ~ " . . . [S]hepherd the flock of God that is among you, exercising oversight, not under compulsion, but willingly, as God would have you; not for shameful gain, but eagerly; not domineering over those in your charge, but being examples to the flock. And when the chief Shepherd appears, you will receive the unfading crown of glory."

Proverbs 1:1-33 ESV ~ "The proverbs of Solomon, son of David, king of Israel: To know wisdom and instruction, to understand words of insight, to receive instruction in wise dealing, in righteousness, justice, and equity; to give prudence to the simple, knowledge and discretion to the youth—Let the wise hear and increase in learning, and the one who understands obtain guidance, . . ."

Prayer
Mentoring God,
You have been our example and have instructed us in Your Word. We ask that You give us the opportunity to mentor others to both share what we know and lead them in the right direction to be the next generation of mentors. Amen.

Reflections from Week 9

1. The ways to make a difference I liked best this week were:

    ☐ Day 57   ☐ Day 60   ☐ Day 63
    ☐ Day 58   ☐ Day 61
    ☐ Day 59   ☐ Day 62

2. Do you have friends or neighbors who travel? Did you offer to help watch over their house and plants while they were away?

3. Did you spend some time with a friend cooking? Were you together or did you do it virtually? Was it fun, challenging, rewarding, or difficult? Will you do it again?

4. To whom did you write a thank you note? Why were you thanking them?

5. Do you grow flowers? Do you have enough to share? Did you share some at the retirement home close to you? What was the reaction?

6. Did you have a get-well card on hand? To whom did you send it? How do *you* feel when you get a card wishing you a speedy recovery?

7. How did you pay it forward?

8. Have you ever been a mentor? Why did you volunteer to do this? What topic did you help someone understand? If you haven't mentored someone, would you consider it?

9. Were you inspired to do something additional to the seven items for this week and, if so, what did you do?

10. List some of the ways you felt while you were making a difference this week.

VOLUNTEER AT A FOOD PANTRY OR A FOOD DISTRIBUTION.

THE FIRST FOOD distribution I volunteered for was the one our church sponsored to celebrate its 50th Anniversary. We had a *lot* of food—a semi-truck full! And a lot of volunteers. The second food distribution site was about 20 miles away, and again, the food was plentiful. Hundreds of people were served, so by the end of each day, all the food was gone. Most communities have a great need for food and helpers to distribute it.

The food that was given out included a lot of fresh fruits and vegetables, frozen meat, dairy products, and even some snack items. Seeing all the fresh produce was wonderful because we added positively to the recipients' nutrition while filling their stomachs.

The many helpers went right to work after prayer and instructions were given. It was amazing to watch everyone as they packaged up the food. Everyone was intent on their particular task, knowing every item needed to be packed in bags before the people began to arrive. It was like a well oiled machine, even with workers who hadn't helped before. Those with experience worked with new folks they had just met. God had work for us to do, and we accomplished His work.

As the cars arrived, I looked at the faces of the recipients and my heart was touched. They were all so grateful for what we were doing. Their struggles to feed their families were set aside for a few days until the contributions were consumed.

If you have an opportunity to volunteer at a food pantry or food distribution, do so. Your heart will be glad you did and you'll know you made a difference in many people's lives in just one day!

"By being kind, we have the power of making the world a happier place in which to live, or at least we greatly diminish the amount of unhappiness in it so as to make it a quite different world."
~ LAWRENCE G. LOVASIK, *THE HIDDEN POWER OF KINDNESS*

"Loving your neighbor means helping those in need
even if they don't live next door!"
~ VEGGIE TALES

Psalm 107:9 ~ "For he satisfies the thirsty, and the hungry he fills
with good things."

I John 2:17 ~ "And the world and its desire are passing away, but
those who do the will of God live forever."

Prayer
Generous God,
As the need for food is great, make us workers for Your kingdom by
helping the many in need. Use our hands to do Your work by feeding
the hungry. Amen.

DAY 7 (65 overall): YOUR COMMUNITY

READ TO A CHILD.

I LOVED READING to my children and now I read to my grandchildren. I always do it right before bed to help settle them down
and have one-on-one time with them. I have quite a few books for
them to choose from, or if they are young, I will select one that's
short enough to keep their interest. As they start school and begin
to read, we take turns; they will read one page and I will read the
next. Literacy in our children, whether they are ours or children
in our community, can bring about change. Reading enriches our
lives. To share it by going into the elementary school and reading
to the students or tutoring students in reading can help both the
children of your community and the other individuals.

The benefits of reading to and with a child are many. From the
beginning of their lives, sitting on a lap with someone reading to
them, makes them feel secure, helps with brain development, and
teaches them basic sounds and words. As they grow, it develops
their imagination and a longer attention span as the story unfolds.

It also encourages speaking and communication skills. Reading teaches them an appreciation for all types of books and their benefits for themselves and the world around them, encouraging them to be life-long readers and learners.[46]

Start a habit of reading to children in your community every chance you get. Reading can make a priceless difference in their lives and yours.

Reading to some of my grandchildren

"One child, one teacher, one pen,
and one book can change the world."
~ Malala Yousafzai

"Reading is a passport to countless adventures."
~ Mary Pope Osborne

2 Timothy 3:14-15 ESV ~ "But as for you, continue in what you have learned and have firmly believed, knowing from whom you

learned it and how from childhood you have been acquainted with the sacred writings, which are able to make you wise for salvation through faith in Christ Jesus."

Romans 15:4 ESV ~ "For whatever was written in former days was written for our instruction, that through endurance and through the encouragement of the Scriptures we might have hope."

Prayer
God the Creator of language,
You created us to communicate with You and with others. As we share the written word of the *Holy Bible* and other books with our children, help us to encourage them to read and learn about You and Your love for them. Help us to encourage them to love books and reading so the world opens up for them. Amen.

DAY 8 (66 overall): YOUR COMMUNITY

HELP WEED A GARDEN IN YOUR COMMUNITY.

THE GARDEN CLUB I've belonged to since 1980 has been maintaining gardens in two locations in our city. We decide which plants go into each garden, prune, deadhead (remove spent blooms), fertilize, and of course, weed. Because these two gardens are in different locations in our city, they impact the neighborhoods differently. One is in a residential area and the other is surrounding a public swimming pool entrance. However, no matter which garden we're working in, someone always stops and thanks us or tells us how pretty the gardens are.

Weeding can be very therapeutic! I feel a great sense of accomplishment when I yank out weeds and fill up my bin. It also gives me an excuse to be outside enjoying nature.

The garden looks so nice when we're finished, and I'm sure the plants thank us because the weeds can no longer steal their nutrients and moisture. Plus, if the weeds grow tall enough, they shade the plants we want there, depriving them of sun, which is also an essential element each plant needs. Weeds can harbor pests or cover up pest activity on the plants, too, making the plants quite vulnerable to pest infestation.

The community benefits from having a beautiful garden close by. Gardens can improve morale, increase property values, inspire the neighbors to improve their yards, and give them a place to walk and enjoy a wide variety of plants. A homeowner across the street from one of the gardens told us, "Every morning as I'm waking up, I roll over, look out the window, and see this beautiful garden. That is the best way to start my day." The impact of a beautiful garden, free of weeds, can make a difference in many ways.

Weeding a garden in our community with our masks on during the pandemic

"I say, if your knees aren't green by the end of the day,
you ought to really re-examine your life."
~ Calvin in *Calvin & Hobbes* by cartoonist Bill Watterson
on finding the joys in life

"I truly believe that somewhere inside of each and every one of us,
we want to make the world a better place."
~ RHETT POWER, *THE ENTREPRENEUR'S BOOK OF ACTIONS*

Song of Solomon 2:12 ESV ~ "The flowers appear on the earth, the
time of singing has come, and the voice of the turtledove is heard in
our land."

1 Corinthians 4:2 ESV ~ "Moreover, it is required of stewards that
they be found trustworthy."

Prayer
God of beauty,
As a garden grows, highlighting the beauty You created, give us the
energy to maintain the gardens by pulling weeds, taking off spent
blooms, and watching out for pests. Help us share the garden's
beauty with others, enhancing their lives and those around them.
Amen.

DAY 9 (67 overall): YOUR COMMUNITY

SHARE YOUR LOVE OF GARDENING (OR OTHER CRAFT).

PLEASE KNOW THAT I encourage you to share your love of any
skill, craft, or interest. Mine just happens to be gardening, so here I
bring to bear my own experiences, many of which you can transfer
to other areas.

If you, too, have a love of gardening, whether it involves flowers, shrubs, vegetables, or herbs, plant the seed (pardon the pun) of
a love of gardening in others. You can begin with young children.

1. **Help Brownies and Girl Scouts with a gardening badge.**
2. **Start a gardening project at a local school.** My sister is a
   master gardener and leads all the kids at her local elementary school in gardening. Each grade has its own garden

plot, and each plot is planted with different plants. They start the seeds, nurture the seedlings, plant them in the plot, and weed their garden. When they begin to harvest, the school cook uses the produce in the lunches for the children. Families come and tend the gardens in the summer. This marvelous gardening project has received grants and many awards.

3. **Lead a homeschool group in gardening.** In the summer of the year my youngest daughter was seven, I had back problems and needed to keep her busy without a lot of physical input on my part. We had planted some Lollipop zinnias earlier that spring. They were up and growing, so I made a simple chart for her to fill in while she was checking on her flowers:
    - How many plants are there?
    - How tall are the plants? (I gave her a yardstick to measure.)
    - How many flowers are blooming?
    - What colors are the flowers?
    - How wide is the biggest flower?
    - Are there any bugs on the plants?
    - She kept her chart and went out each week to fill in the answers. You can use this idea of a chart if you lead a group or a child in gardening or another interest.

4. **Teach a community gardening class for adults.** Sharing your love of gardening could inspire many people to become garden lovers as well.

A lovely memorial garden at my church

Sharing your love of gardening with children could make a difference now and for many years to come as they grow older.

"The talents we each have been blessed with can only be
developed if we use them fully to benefit the lives
of others as well as our own."
~ KAREN CASEY, *THE PROMISE OF A NEW DAY*

"To plant a garden is to believe in tomorrow."
~ AUDREY HEPBURN (1929-1993)

Exodus 35:31 ~ ". . . [H]e has filled him with divine spirit, with skill, intelligence, and knowledge in every kind of craft, . . ."

Philippians 1:6 ~ "I am confident of this, that the one who began a good work among you will bring it to completion by the day of Jesus Christ."

Prayer
Blessed Lord God,
For those of us who love gardening, thank You. As we share that love, help us also share our knowledge, time, and plants or seeds.

Help us nurture a love in others as we nurture our plants. All of this helps us get closer to You by loving what You have created. Amen.

DAY 10 (68 overall): YOUR COMMUNITY

HELP SOMEONE IN THE GROCERY STORE WHILE YOU ARE SHOPPING.

MANY OF YOU may be doing these simple acts already.

1. If a shorter person can't reach something on the top shelf, offer to get it for them.
2. If someone looks lost, ask them if they need help.
3. If someone asks you where something is located, walk with them, and show them.
4. If you have an extra coupon you aren't going to use, share it.
5. All in all, be kind to someone who needs help and do what you can.

Here's a story by someone who has experienced both sides of the coin.

Reciprocal Kindness

I'm a man of 82 who walks with a cane because of a spinal issue, but I usually do the grocery shopping for our household. I like to get out, get a little exercise, and see other people. Several times, I've had the opportunity to help shoppers who can't reach the high shelves in the grocery store. On one occasion, I was the recipient of such help. I wanted raisins, and the last raisin box was in the back of the bottom shelf, but I couldn't bend down sufficiently to reach it. A woman came along and offered to be of assistance, and we worked as a team to solve the problem. I hooked the raisin box with my cane and pulled it forward, and she bent down and got it for me. It's a good feeling to help—and to be helped as well. We're all in life together. We might as well make it easier for one another. ~ John Clayton

One simple gesture, whether you give or receive it, can make a difference.

"Go out and make a difference in your community. You don't need endless time and perfect conditions. Do it now. Do it today. Do it for twenty minutes and watch your heart start beating."
~ BARBARA SHER (1935-2020)

Proverbs 22:9 ~ "Those who are generous are blessed, for they share their bread with the poor."

I Timothy 6:18 ~ "They are to do good, to be rich in good works, generous, and ready to share, . . ."

Prayer
Faithful God,
You supply all our needs, whether You give us a job so we can buy our own groceries or perhaps help out others in need of a job who don't have enough money to buy their own groceries. For the opportunities You have given us or put in our path, thank You. Amen.

DAY 11 (69 overall): YOUR COMMUNITY

SHARE A PLANT OR AN HERB FROM YOUR GARDEN.

I LOVE HERBS and began my herb business in 1983. Some plants seed themselves and spread out each year, so I need to divide or transplant them each spring. I love to share those new plants with people in my community.

My garden club sponsored a plant exchange for many years. People brought extra plants from their garden and exchanged them for plants others brought. No money required. We also have a plant auction fundraiser in June where people can bid on our plants and take them home for a good price. Sometimes people bring freebies and just hand them out.

I've also seen people put plants out by the street with a FREE sign. However you want to do it, just share from your abundance. It could make a difference.

The legacy garden of a friend, in which all the plants were given to him by others

"Giving back to society and community enriches our lives,
making it a double blessing."
~ Kellie Sullivan

I look at my friend's garden as a triple blessing. It's a blessing for those who shared the plants, for my friend who created a lovely garden with those plants, and for all the passersby who have the privilege of looking at the beautiful garden he designed and planted.

"We might think we are nurturing our garden,
but of course it's our garden that is really nurturing us."
~ Jenny Uglow

Job 12:8 ~ "... [A]sk the plants of the earth, and they will teach you; and the fish of the sea will declare to you."

James 1:17 ~ "Every generous act of giving, with every perfect gift, is from above, coming down from the Father of lights, with whom there is no variation or shadow due to change."

Prayer
God of all things beautiful,
As we grow the beautiful plants that You created in our gardens, remind us of their beauty and to share them with others to spread that beauty around. Amen.

DAY 12 (70 overall): YOUR COMMUNITY

INVITE SOMEONE TO CHURCH.

WHAT IS THE risk? The worst thing that could happen is they say "No." The best thing that could happen is they say "Yes," and you had a part in changing their future.

By inviting someone to attend, you have planted the seed, but it's up to the Holy Spirit to work on their heart. Over 30 years ago, a person I knew but hadn't seen for years crossed my path again. I invited her to church and told her about the church and our minister. The following Sunday she didn't come, and I was disappointed. However, she came the next Sunday and has come every Sunday since. I can't tell you all the projects she's worked on and the help she has given to the church using her time and talents. It just took a simple act of planting the seed and turning the rest over to the Lord.

Jeff Noble *(Notes from the Trail)* gives us five reasons to invite someone to church.[47]

1. **"They will more than likely come."** A study showed that "96 *percent* of the unchurched are at least somewhat likely to attend church if they are invited.[48] . . .

2. **"Inviting someone else will usher you into spiritual adventure.** When you don't invite or play a role in the invitational process, you think you're playing it safe. No harm done. Right? But you're missing out on one of life's most incredible opportunities — being able to play a role in someone's life transformation. Being used by God to introduce someone to forgiveness, peace, and ultimate purpose?! There's nothing more rewarding or energizing! . . .

3. **"It will challenge you to refresh your heart, your knowledge and your living.** When we take steps to intentionally invite someone to church, we often go through a self-evaluation. . . .

4. **"It will give the people you invite the opportunity to make a more *informed* decision about church and Jesus and eternity.** Prior to your invitation, they are making assessments based on what they've heard, on the media, and other portrayals of religion. Give them an opportunity to rethink things from personal experience and trust God with the process. . . .

5. **"It will make you see your church in a whole new light, and you can share what you observe.** Nothing is better for taking blinders off than when you have a guest present. You realize the welcome and announcement time isn't done very well. You see misspelled words on the projection screen. You notice that your church family actually is (or isn't) welcoming. You hear the sermon as if it's your first one. You're on edge, experiencing everything through the eyes and ears of your guest."

The sanctuary of my church

For all these reasons, you could make a difference—not just for the near future, but for eternity.

"The more we care for the happiness of others,
the greater our own sense of well-being becomes."
~ THE DALAI LAMA

"A small act is worth a million thoughts."
~ AI WEIWE

James 4:2 ~ "You do not have, because you do not ask."

Proverbs 9:9 ~ "Instruct the wise and they will be wiser still; teach the righteous and they will add to their learning."

Prayer
Lord God,
Give us courage to invite someone to church. Working on their heart is Your job but let us begin with a simple invitation. As we approach this person, ready their heart to accept the invitation and change their life. Amen.

Reflections from Week 10

1. The ways to make a difference I liked best this week were:

   ☐ Day 64   ☐ Day 67   ☐ Day 70
   ☐ Day 65   ☐ Day 68
   ☐ Day 66   ☐ Day 69

2. If you volunteered at a food pantry or food distribution, why did you help, what did you do, and whom did you service?
3. What child did you read to? What book did you read? Did you take turns reading?
4. Have you ever helped in a garden in your community? When did you do this? Will you do it again?
5. Have you taught any classes on crafts or gardening to others who are interested? What did you teach? How did it go?
6. This week did you assist someone in the grocery store who was having trouble reaching or finding something? What was their reaction?
7. Have you ever shared a plant with someone? Did you do it this week? Did you give instructions?
8. Did you invite someone to church this week? Did they come? Did you pick them up or did they come by themselves?
9. Were you inspired to do something additional to the seven items for this week and, if so, what did you do?
10. List some of the ways you felt while you were making a difference this week.

CLEAN UP A NEIGHBORHOOD PARK WITH OTHERS OR CLEAN UP AN AREA TO MAKE A PARK.

MANY COMMUNITIES RECLAIM a forgotten park that is over-grown with weeds and full of trash and has broken playground equipment. You and others in your community can make the park vibrant again. A park is great for a variety of beneficial activities for all who use it.

Clean up whatever doesn't belong in the park, such as trash, bottles, cans, and broken tree limbs. Every park needs some trees for shade. If there are already trees and bushes there, prune them and give them a fresh start. If it's bare, work up a simple landscape design and plant a few trees as a start. Create a play area. Put a new coat of paint on any equipment that's already there, and paint hopscotch squares on the pavement, or paint a mural on a wall. Make minor repairs on any equipment, light fixtures, basketball hoops, and so on. Add trash and recycling bins if needed. Build a few benches if there aren't any, or put a fresh coat of paint on the ones that are there. You can even create a spot for a community garden.[49]

Have a fundraiser to cover the costs for your plan. If you have a specific plan and have researched the costs for each item, people will be more willing to contribute. A fundraiser such as an ice cream social can bring the community together for this good cause.

Get involved in cleaning up a park and make a difference in your community and for everyone who visits.

"We must remember that one determined person can make a significant difference, and that a small group of determined people can change the course of history."
~ SONIA JOHNSON

"Give it your all. Whatever work you do,
do it to the best of your ability."
~ Jerry Dorsman and Bob Davis,
How to Achieve Peace of Mind

Philippians 4:8 ESV ~ "Finally, brothers, whatever is true, whatever is honorable, whatever is just, whatever is pure, whatever is lovely, whatever is commendable, if there is any excellence, if there is anything worthy of praise, think about these things."

Proverbs 21:5 ~ "The plans of the diligent lead surely to abundance, but everyone who is hasty comes only to want."

Prayer
All-knowing God,
We come to You today for You know what our community needs. Help us discern what that is and work toward that goal. Be it a park, a community garden, or a playground, give us the insight to know the needs, make a plan, and complete that project. Amen.

DAY 14 (72 overall): YOUR COMMUNITY

SHARE YOUR LOVE OF EDUCATION WITH A CHILD.

Compare the enthusiasm of a child attending school for the first time to a 14-year-old in middle school. What happened to change that enthusiasm? A stronger community is an educated community. What can you do to help? Read to the kids in school, volunteer to tutor in the classroom. Kids are naturally thirsty for knowledge. Help develop that by answering their questions and making them curious.

Parents could be encouraged to learn basic principles to help their child hang on to that early enthusiasm. For example, they need to talk to their children in positive ways to keep that pre-school enthusiasm alive. They can encourage children to follow through and complete their projects, and if they don't do as well as they could, help them learn from their mistakes and do better next time. Remember, playing outdoors is educational, too. Children may need a break to unwind so they can then attack their school-work with renewed enthusiasm.[50]

I remember when my three girls were babies, I talked to them all the time. Later, we counted things at the store, read labels, and did things that got them interested in the world around them, making learning fun. They succeeded in school and now are raising children of their own. Set an example for your children by reading for pleasure and assisting them when they need a little push—not doing the work for them, but helping them over little speed bumps.

A love of learning opens innumerable doors for your children. Invest your time and energy into planting the seeds of learning in your children early on and you'll all reap the benefits for a lifetime. You can make a measurable difference to enrich each of their lives.

> "You were born to make a difference, to contribute
> and to share your gifts with the world."
> ~ DARREN HARDY

Your World
Georgia Douglas Johnson (1880-1966)

Your world is as big as you make it.
I know, for I used to abide
In the narrowest nest in a corner,
My wings pressing close to my side.
But I sighted the distant horizon
Where the skyline encircled the sea
And I throbbed with a burning desire
To travel this immensity.
I battered the cordons around me
And cradled my wings on the breeze,

Then soared to the uttermost reaches
With rapture, with power, with ease![51]

Deuteronomy 4:9 ~ "But take care and watch yourselves closely, so as neither to forget the things that your eyes have seen nor to let them slip from your mind all the days of your life; make them known to your children and your children's children...."

Proverbs 3:1-2 ~ "My child, do not forget my teaching, but let your heart keep my commandments; for length of days and years of life and abundant welfare they will give you."

Prayer

Creator God,
As we assist in our children's education, help us create an atmosphere for learning so they have successes that will positively impact their future. We want to raise successful citizens for our communities and the world. Amen.

DAY 15 (73 overall): YOUR COMMUNITY

MAKE A DOOR DECORATION FOR A NURSING HOME RESIDENT.

TAP INTO YOUR creative juices and make a door decoration or two for a nursing home resident. It can be as simple as taking an old calendar and framing one of the beautiful photographs to hang on their door. You could even give them all 12 photographs with the frame so they could insert a new one every month. Or, you could have a photo for each of the four seasons or celebrate a special holiday each month.

If you need help with this project, ask the youth group at your church or one of the other organizations you might belong to. This is a great outreach project that would make the residents feel special and make a difference for them in knowing somebody cared about them.

"How many times in our lives do we stand at the threshold of making a difference? We evaluate the options and decide whether we want to get involved or just turn a blind eye and head home. Daily, it seems, we face numerous chances to make somebody's life a little easier, even if it means ours may be a little more difficult. One of the commitments I am making is to be the stranger who serves."
~ MARTY CAULEY, DYING TO GO ON VACATION

"We have all known the long loneliness and we have learned that the only solution is love and that love comes with community."
~ DOROTHY DAY (1897-1980), JOURNALIST AND SOCIAL ACTIVIST

I John 4:11 ~ "Beloved, since God loved us so much, we also ought to love one another."

Micah 6:8 ~ "He has told you, O mortal, what is good; and what does the Lord require of you but to do justice, and to love kindness, and to walk humbly with your God?"

Prayer
Caring Jesus,
As we move through this life, help us think and care about others, especially those who may not have anyone else to do nice things for them. Encourage us to come up with a project that would make those people feel special and, in the process, create empathy in us. Amen.

DAY 16 (74 overall): YOUR COMMUNITY

DONATE BLOOD.

HAVE YOU EVER saved a life? This is one of the easiest things to do to make a difference. I have been donating blood for over 10 years. I never considered it earlier in my life. My youngest daughter, a nurse, got me started when she brought me with her. There have been times in the last 10 years when I couldn't donate, such as after surgery or when I wasn't feeling well. I know I made up excuses why I shouldn't—until I started and found it so easy. To me, the worst part was answering all those questions. Now you can answer them online and save all sorts of time.

Why should you donate?

1. Blood can't be manufactured; it must come from another human.
2. One out of every seven hospital patients will need a transfusion.
3. A one-hour donation could save three people's lives.
4. Your body replaces the blood you donated quickly so you can donate every eight weeks.
5. Donating repeatedly can improve how your blood flows through vessels and can significantly reduce your risk of a heart attack.
6. Only 37 percent of the American population is eligible to donate and only 10 percent of those people do donate.
7. The need is great.
8. You may need blood at some time in your life.
9. You get a free mini-physical: They take your temperature, pulse, and blood pressure and check your hemoglobin level.
10. You'll have personal satisfaction knowing you can make a difference and may even save a life with your very lifeblood.

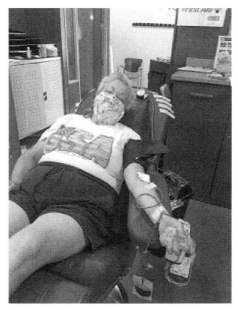

Me donating blood

"Not all of us can do great things.
But we can do small things with great love."
~ MOTHER TERESA (1910-1997)

"One life can make a difference, you see, it's up to you!"
~ AUTHOR UNKNOWN, *JUST ONE*

2 Corinthians 9:7 ESV ~ "Each one must give as he has decided in his heart, not reluctantly or under compulsion, for God loves a cheerful giver."

Luke 6:38 ~ ". . . [I]t will be given to you. A good measure, pressed down, shaken together, running over, will be put into your lap; for the measure you give will be the measure you get back."

Prayer
God, the Great Physician,
Thank You for making our bodies so mysterious and wonderful. The

fact that we can save lives with a blood donation, and our blood regenerates itself in days is miraculous. Encourage others to do this life-saving activity. Amen.

DAY 17 (75 overall): YOUR COMMUNITY

HELP LOCAL BUSINESSES BY SHOPPING THERE.

DURING THE PANDEMIC, it was important for us to support the local businesses in our community— and it still is for several reasons. It helps create jobs in the community, which in turn helps the local economy. In addition, with taxes, 68 percent of that money goes back into the community for schools, libraries, and parks.

By shopping at local businesses, you show them your support, and they in turn help support groups such as Little League teams and charities such as soup kitchens. Plus, local businesses don't necessarily stock their shelves with the same things chain stores do; therefore, you can find special gifts that aren't available elsewhere.[52]

Shop locally to help mom-and-pop stores thrive. You can make a difference not only in the lives of the shop owners, but in your community, because most of the shop owners live in the community they serve.

One of the family-owned markets in my community

"There are a countless number of opportunities
where we can make a difference every day."
~ CATHERINE PULSIFER, *YOU CAN MAKE A DIFFERENCE*

"When you buy from a small business, you're not helping a
CEO buy a third vacation home. You are helping a little girl
get dance lessons, a little boy his team jersey, a mom put food on
the table, a dad pay a mortgage, or a student pay for college."
~ ANONYMOUS

Acts 19:25 ~ "These he gathered together, with the workers of the
same trade, and said, 'Men, you know that we get our wealth from
this business.'"

James 4:13 ~ "Come now, you who say, 'Today or tomorrow we
will go to such and such a town and spend a year there, doing
business and making money.'"

Prayer
God of prosperity,
Remind us to shop locally to help our community and the businesses
therein. Thus, we reward the entrepreneurial spirit you have given
the shopkeepers and small-business owners and help our community
thrive. Amen.

DAY 18 (76 overall): YOUR COMMUNITY

PARTICIPATE IN "GOD'S WORK, OUR HANDS" OR SIMILAR ORGANIZATIONS.

FOR MANY YEARS, I have participated with other members of
Evangelical Lutheran Churches of America across the country in
"God's Work, Our Hands." People in need of help, whether they're
individuals or nonprofits, notify agencies of their need, and we
gather and work to make their lives and environment better. Over
the years, I have painted fences and furnace rooms, cleaned out

stairwells, cut and removed dead tree limbs, and weeded. Organizers from church have filled kids' backpacks with school supplies and new pairs of shoes.

In the flood of May 2020, our community and neighboring communities were hit hard and in need of help. So, about 50 of our church members went into an area to clean up. Houses had been swept away and debris from those houses and houses upstream was left behind and needed to be cleaned up. The area was to be made into a park. We spent several hours filling black garbage bags, piling wood (both trees and planks from houses), and piling other debris so the heavy equipment could scoop it up and carry it away.

When I arrived, I had no idea it was so bad. When I found a swimsuit top half buried in sand, it hit me that this is where people had lived and the house they had loved was no longer there. The work we did was a drop in the bucket compared to what needed to be done and had already been done—but lots of drops can fill that bucket and make a difference.

Cleaning up after the May 2020 flood in Midland, Michigan

"Be thankful when you're tired and weary,
because it means you've made a difference."
~ Author Unknown

"If we believe that tomorrow will be better,
we can bear a hardship today."
~ THICH NHAT HANH (1926-2022)

James 2:14-17 ESV ~ "What good is it, my brothers, if someone says he has faith but does not have works? Can that faith save him? If a brother or sister is poorly clothed and lacking in daily food, and one of you says to them, 'Go in peace, be warmed and filled,' without giving them the things needed for the body, what good is that? So also faith by itself, if it does not have works, is dead."

Matthew 5:16 ESV ~ "In the same way, let your light shine before others, so that they may see your good works and give glory to your Father who is in heaven."

Prayer

Compassionate God,
Share Your spirit of compassion with us so we can help those in desperate need. Use our hands to do Your work and accomplish more than we could on our own. Amen.

DAY 19 (77 overall): YOUR COMMUNITY

HELP SERVE AT A SOUP KITCHEN OR COMMUNITY THANKSGIVING MEAL.

YEARS AGO, I helped serve a Thanksgiving meal for the needy, and just recently, I served lunch at the Open Door, a soup kitchen in our community. The experience at the Open Door was eye opening. The organizational skills of the people in charge were amazing. The food comes in from many different places, and they needed to put it to good use in a timely fashion and come up with creative ways to combine the foods. Sandwich lunches were served in paper bags outside as well as hot lunch inside.[53]

Preparing food and serving lunch at the Open Door

It was a rewarding experience, meeting the people we worked with and the people we served. Every experience is educational. We learned life skills, built relationships, and gave back to those in need while learning about their needs.

Your local soup kitchens are always in need of volunteers, so help out and make a difference. If you engage in this kind of service as a family, it makes a difference in your family as well. It helps you all appreciate your blessings, builds family bonds, and sets a good example for one another.

"Why should there be hunger and deprivation in any land, in any city, at any table, when man has the resources and the scientific know-how to provide all mankind with the basic necessities of life? There is no deficit in human resources. The deficit is in human will."
~ MARTIN LUTHER KING JR.

"Food is national security. Food is economy.
It is employment, energy, history. Food is everything."
~ CHEF JOSÉ ANDRÉS, FOUNDER OF WORLD CENTRAL KITCHEN

Deuteronomy 15:7 ~ "If there is among you anyone in need, a member of your community in any of your towns within the land that the Lord your God is giving you, do not be hard-hearted or tight-fisted toward your needy neighbor."

And don't forget about the feeding of the five thousand:

Matthew 14:13-21 ~ "When Jesus heard what had happened, he withdrew by boat privately to a solitary place. Hearing of this, the crowds followed him on foot from the towns. When Jesus landed and saw a large crowd, he had compassion on them and healed their sick. As evening approached, the disciples came to him and said, 'This is a remote place, and it's already getting late. Send the crowds away, so they can go to the villages and buy themselves some food.'

Jesus replied, 'They do not need to go away. You give them something to eat.'

'We have here only five loaves of bread and two fish,' they answered.

'Bring them here to me,' he said. And he directed the people to sit down on the grass. Taking the five loaves and the two fish and looking up to heaven, he gave thanks and broke the loaves. Then he gave them to the disciples, and the disciples gave them to the people. They all ate and were satisfied, and the disciples picked up twelve basketfuls of broken pieces that were left over. The number of those who ate was about five thousand men, besides women and children."

Prayer
Generous God,
Thank You for our blessings and the opportunity to share those blessings with others. Remind us that soup kitchens always need volunteers, and they could use our help regardless of our skill level. Amen.

Reflections from Week 11

1. The ways to make a difference I liked best this week were:

    ☐ Day 71   ☐ Day 74   ☐ Day 77
    ☐ Day 72   ☐ Day 75
    ☐ Day 73   ☐ Day 76

2. Have you ever helped clean up a community park or reclaim an area to put in a park? Where is the park? How many hours did you work at it?
3. Do you love education? Have you shared that love with a child in your community? Who was the child? How did you share your love?
4. Did you make a door decoration for a nursing home resident? What did you make? Where did you get the idea? What was the reaction? Will you do it again?
5. Have you ever donated blood? Why did you start donating or why haven't you donated? What would it take to encourage you to donate?
6. Do you regularly shop locally? Why or why not? What encouragement do you need to shop locally?
7. Has your church worked on a project together to help the community? Why or why not? Would you be willing to organize an event to get them started?
8. This week did you help at a soup kitchen? Where was it located and what did you do while you were there? Will you do it again?
9. Were you inspired to do something additional to the seven items for this week and, if so, what did you do?
10. List some of the ways you felt while you were making a difference this week.

DAY 20 (78 overall): YOUR COMMUNITY

FIX A MEAL FOR A NEW MOTHER AND HER FAMILY.

IF YOU HAVE ever been a new mom or dad you know how stressful bringing home a new baby can be. You are trying to do everything you did before you had the baby, but now this little person takes a lot more time than you anticipated. Having someone in your community bring your family dinner is one less meal you have to think about and prepare.

When I was having babies, other church members were also having babies. We rotated taking meals to one another, knowing how much we all appreciated one less meal to prepare.

Here are some helpful tips on bringing food to a new mom.

1.   Use disposable containers so she doesn't have to return casserole dishes, etc.
2.   Consider bringing plasticware/paperware for eating, making cleanup easy.
3.   Choose healthy options.
4.   Make enough for leftovers.
5.   Ensure it's easy prep so they can eat it right away or easily reheat it.
6.   Write reheating instructions on the container.
7.   Portion the food and package it so the containers can be stored in the freezer and then taken out just a portion at a time to reheat and eat when desired.
8.   If the food will be going into the freezer, write the date, what's inside the container, and reheating or cooking instructions on the outside.

By helping this mother, you are making a difference to a whole family in your community.

"If you want others to be happy, practice compassion.
If you want to be happy, practice compassion."
~ DALAI LAMA

"But you can make a difference, everyone can do that too.
May those who can use the help, receive what they ought to."
~ JULIE HEBERT, *THE CHRISTMAS STAR*

Galatians 5:22-23 ESV ~ "But the fruit of the Spirit is love, joy, peace, patience, kindness, goodness, faithfulness, gentleness, self-control; against such things there is no law."

Matthew 19:19 ~ "Honor your father and mother; also, you shall love your neighbor as yourself."

Prayer
Thoughtful Jesus,
We want to follow Your example and be thoughtful, helping those who need it. Remind us of what it was like when we were a new mom or dad and help us show the new parents kindness and generosity as You would have us do. Amen.

CHAPTER 5

MAKE A DIFFERENCE IN YOUR COUNTRY

THE RIPPLES ARE moving outward. Many of the items in this chapter could be exchanged for ones in a different chapter, depending on how far out your connections travel. Since I moved to Michigan from Minnesota 40-plus years ago, many of my high school and college friends live out of my area. To contact and visit with them is always a blessing. In addition, making contact with strangers in simple ways can be a blessing to us both.

Why Make a Difference in Your Country?
Six good reasons are to:

1. help ensure all people are treated fairly, with caring and justice;
2. help create a safe and free place to live for our children and grandchildren;
3. understand others, help with healing, and keep connections open;
4. help improve the way we operate and interact for more harmony and effectiveness;
5. conserve our natural resources;
6. reduce pollution and lessen landfill input with recycling.

Remember that the good things you do ripple outward. Because you are a citizen of our beautiful country, you help define the nature of our citizens as a whole. *Thank you* for adding to the goodness of our country!

DAY 1 (79 overall): YOUR COUNTRY

SEND A CARD OR EMAIL, MAKE A CALL, OR VISIT AN OLD FRIEND IN PERSON.

It's always good to keep in touch with old friends who may now live far away. Connecting seems to draw the country together. Emails, texts, and social media make it easy to stay in contact if you're computer savvy. However, cards are special and gratifying to receive. I send Christmas cards to several high school friends, but a phone call to hear their voice and have a conversation is even better. It seems the older I get, the more reminiscent I am. That feeling of nostalgia makes me smile. When I remember my formative years and the friends who were a part of that time, I yearn to include them in my memories and where I went after our time together.

Remember the old song "Make new friends but keep the old; one is silver and the other gold"? Connecting with old friends can remind you of who you were, and rediscovering that former "you" may help you discover who you want to be now and what kind of friends you want in your life. With friendships of the past, you'll see how you've all grown, and a small effort on your part can rekindle a valuable friendship.[54] It also expands your support system and theirs. Good people are hard to come by. Make a difference and give that friend a call.

My 50th high school class reunion, a great place to become reacquainted with old friends

"Though miles may lie between us, we're never far apart, for friendship doesn't count the miles, it's measured in the heart."
~ ROZINA HASHAM

"I'm never sad when a friend goes far away, because whichever city or country that friend goes to, they turn the place friendly. They turn a suspicious-looking name on the map into a place where a welcome can be found."
~ HELEN OYEYEMI

Job 2:11 ~ "Now when Job's three friends heard of all these troubles that had come upon him, each of them set out from his home—Eliphaz the Temanite, Bildad the Shuhite, and Zophar the Naamathite. They met together to go and console and comfort him."

III John 1:15 ~ "Peace to you. The friends send you their greetings. Greet the friends there, each by name."

Prayer
Jesus, friend to all,
What a blessing friends are. We can never have too many. As we go through our busy life, help us reconnect with old friends and nurture our relationships with both old and new friends. Amen.

DONATE YOUR EXTRA ITEMS TO SALVATION ARMY, GOODWILL, ETC.

WE ALL HAVE extra clothing, kitchenware, tools, and other items taking up space in our homes that could be used by somebody else who has a need for them.

The older I get, the more this surfeit of items comes to mind. After cleaning out my parents' house and my in-laws' house, I want even more to clean out my own house so my children don't get stuck with that task.

1. I'm always working toward having less "stuff." It makes life simpler and gives me more space to move.
2. Donating my stuff instead of throwing it away keeps it out of landfills and gives it a second chance to be used by someone else.
3. Making donations to a nonprofit is a tax write-off, so it helps my bottom line.
4. The donation facility hires local people to work, so I'm helping to provide jobs.
5. Achieving a simpler lifestyle helps me learn how to let go of things I no longer need, not only physically but psychologically.
6. By giving the items a second chance to be purchased, I'm giving people the opportunity to buy those items at a reduced price from when those items were sold new.

You can feel more at peace with less clutter, help people in your community and beyond, and avoid contributing to landfills, just by dropping off your unwanted things at Goodwill, the Salvation Army, or a similar organization. So, whether you are moving, minimizing, or decluttering your home, donating is a good option that makes a difference.

"The purpose of life is not to be happy – but to matter, to be productive, to be useful, to have it make some difference that you have lived at all."
~ LEO ROSTEN (1908-1997)

"What do we live for, if not to make life less difficult for each other?"
~ GEORGE ELIOT (1819-1880)

Matthew 20:15 ~ "Am I not allowed to do what I choose with what belongs to me? Or are you envious because I am generous?"

II Corinthians 8:7 ~ "Now as you excel in everything—in faith, in speech, in knowledge, in utmost eagerness, and in our love for you—so we want you to excel also in this generous undertaking."

Prayer
Good and Gracious God,
As we declutter our homes, please remind us to donate the things others could use that we no longer need. While we are decluttering our house, help us declutter our entire lives of the unnecessary things that weigh us down. Amen.

DAY 3 (81 overall): YOUR COUNTRY

SMILE AT A STRANGER.

WE TELL OUR children not to talk to strangers, and when my sister lived in New York City, she never made eye contact with anyone.

So please use your commonsense here when I suggest you smile at a stranger. Choose your strangers wisely! Judge where you are and be careful. Here are some people you could bless with a smile:

- A store clerk, waitress, salesman, road worker, traffic controller, flagger, and the like
- The people you come across at the grocery store, doctor's office, etc.
- A frustrated mom trying to comfort an unhappy child
- An elderly person who may be feeling lonely
- Weary (or not-so-weary) travelers and employees helping travelers if you're traveling around the country

Mother Teresa once said, "I'll never understand all the good that a simple smile can accomplish." Smiling at a stranger . . .

1. can bring pleasure into your life and that of the other person;
2. can be good for your soul, changing your disposition for the day—and probably the other person's as well;
3. makes you more attractive by being positive and can uplift the people to whom you give a smile;
4. can spread to a lot of people by rippling outward, so just think how many may be impacted by a simple smile from you that others catch and pass on;
5. shows another person they have value.[55]

It was Robert Harling who said that a smile "increases your face value." So smile; it can make a difference.

Smiling at a stranger

"Smile, it is the key that fits the lock of everybody's heart."
~ ANTHONY J. D'ANGELO (1924-2006)

"Peace begins with a smile."
~ MOTHER TERESA (1910-1997)

Romans 12:13 ~ "Contribute to the needs of the saints; extend hospitality to strangers."

Job 29:24 ~ "I smiled on them when they had no confidence; and the light of my countenance they did not extinguish."

Prayer
Joyful Savior,
As we go through our day, help us remember to smile at others. Reveal their need to us for a little joy, acknowledgment of their existence, and a small pleasantry from another human. Amen.

ENCOURAGE SOMEONE TO CONTINUE WORKING ON A SPECIAL PROJECT.

WHETHER THE PROJECT is writing a book, singing in 100 gardens, painting a picture, photographing flowers, or cooking your way through *Mastering the Art of French Cooking*, your encouragement could make a difference in them and the completion of their project.

My friend Chuck Voigt has a goal of singing in 100 gardens. I asked for his input to be included in my book for this day.

"How is it going?" I asked.

"It was really catching some momentum last summer and fall, and I had high hopes for additional trips to New England and back to Minnesota this spring and summer, but all that went by the wayside with the COVID-19 situation, so the effort is basically stalled, pending a new way of looking at and doing it."

"When did you decide to do this?"

"As I was retiring, I kept getting the question, 'What are you going to do now that you're retired?' One day it popped into my head to say, 'I want to sing in one hundred gardens!' That was almost five years ago now."

"Why did you decide to do this?"

"I love gardens, travel, and singing, so what could be a better goal? Given my cancer issues and having heard the words, 'You will not be able to sing after radiation,' and living with that expectation for months, it felt like a worthwhile mission to celebrate the fact that that pronouncement didn't come to pass."

"What kind of encouragement have you received from others?"

"All my IHA (International Herb Association) friends (and many others) were supportive, but it was the nudging from Susan Belsinger that finally got me going. In 2018, she forced the issue in Arkansas, where I recorded the first two songs. You, too, helped out, as have Jim Long, Theresa Mieseler, Carolee Snyder, and others. No one ever said, 'What a stupid idea!' which sort of confirmed I was on the right track."

"What kind of a difference did that encouragement make?"

"What Susan did to get the first one recorded forced me out of my head and into forward gear. That grew to having sixteen gardens on my 'done' list. After the shutdown, I did the additional one in my daffodil patch. That was helped by my cousin Jill, who came and shot the videos, despite having heard that her younger sister had been found dead in her apartment in Boulder, Colorado. She never let on until after we had finished; then she told my sister Donna and me the news and broke down. My mission was that important to her. She has volunteered to take me to other gardens around home to sing and keep the ball rolling, and I may take her up on it."

As you can see, encouraging others really does make a difference!

My friend Chuck, singing in my garden during 2019,
when our garden/yard was on the Midland Garden Walk

"Joy can be real only if people look upon their lives as a service and have a definite object in life outside themselves and their personal happiness."
~ Leo Tolstoy (1828-1910)

"It may amaze you to see what potential people can reach when they receive words that reassure them that they are on the right track. Positive words can truly make a difference in the lives of others, more than you may realize."
~ Catherine Pulsifer, *A Gift of Value*

I Thessalonians 4:18 ~ "Therefore encourage one another with these words."

Acts 11:21-26 ~ "The hand of the Lord was with them, and a great number became believers and turned to the Lord. News of this came to the ears of the church in Jerusalem, and they sent Barnabas to Antioch. When he came and saw the grace of God, he rejoiced, and he exhorted them all to remain faithful to the Lord with steadfast devotion; for he was a good man, full of the Holy Spirit and of faith. And a great many people were brought to the Lord. Then Barnabas went to Tarsus to look for Saul, and when he had found him, he brought him to Antioch. So it was that for an entire year they met with the church and taught a great many people, and it was in Antioch that the disciples were first called 'Christians.'"

Prayer
Encouraging God,
As we encounter people in our lives who are thinking about or working on a special project, help us encourage them to begin or complete that project. May we take the time needed to reinforce their value, giving them the boost they need. Amen.

BE THE LIGHT AND KINDLY SHOW SOMEONE HOW TO DO SOMETHING.

REMEMBER, WE ALL need help at some point. It's very frustrating when we get stuck in the middle of something and don't know what to do next.

How can you help? To begin with, you need to be a good listener so you know when others *need* your help. Second, you need to convince them they can do it with a little help. Third, you need to respectfully guide them along the way and not desert them partway through. Acknowledge their vulnerability (to yourself) and be sympathetic to their situation.

Be the light: Shine your light on others to make their life brighter. It doesn't mean you have to be perfect and always blissfully happy. No one is like that.

This quotation from Susie Draper explains: "It means doing things that make me feel free and peaceful, surrendering control, trusting my intuition, showing compassion and kindness to myself and others, and believing the simple truth that I am enough. It is about bringing light to the places that are dark."[56]

To be the light, you will look for opportunities to lift someone else up. You'll make a conscious effort to do the things you know make your own light shine brighter so you can also help other people recognize the light within them. What you admire in others is often a recognition of the same thing within you, so the light you see in others is a reflection of your own light.

Think of yourself as a lighthouse, sending out beacons to guide someone else's way so they get to the harbor safely. That makes a difference.

"There are two ways of spreading light; to be the candle or the mirror that reflects it."
~ EDITH WHARTON (1862-1937)

"Know what sparks the light in you.
Then use that light to illuminate the world."
~ Oprah Winfrey

Isaiah 42:16 ~ "I will lead the blind by a road they do not know, by paths they have not known I will guide them. I will turn the darkness before them into light, the rough places into level ground. These are the things I will do, and I will not forsake them."

Ephesians 5:8b-9 ~ "Live as children of light—for the fruit of the light is found in all that is good and right and true."

Prayer
Jesus the Light,
Guide our path to point out when others could use our knowledge. We don't want to be in the way, but we do want to help them. Help us discern the situation so we can listen and encourage them in the way they need. Amen.

DAY 6 (84 overall): YOUR COUNTRY

VOTE.

Every year we have Election Day. It's your right and responsibility to cast your vote, whether in person or by mail. You may say, "I'm only one person, so what difference does it make if I vote or not?" Your vote may decide the winner:

In Ohio alone, 14 races for office in 2015 resulted in either a tie or a single-vote margin, according to the *Record-Courier* newspaper.

Six other times in various states, the results were determined by one vote:[57]

1. 1910 election for the 36th Congressional District of New York
2. 2000 Seat Pleasant, Maryland, mayoral election

3. 2008 Alaska House of Representatives District 7 election
4. 2012 Democratic primary for 87th legislative district in Missouri
5. 2013 election for 12th legislative district in New York
6. 2017 Clyman, Wisconsin, board chairman

So, make a difference and VOTE.

"Collectively, votes matter a great deal. Certain groups in the population that have higher turnout rates—such as older voters, the wealthy, and white Americans—benefit from the clout that they achieve as a result."
~ SEAN MCELWEE, AN ANALYST

"We all like to be acknowledged and appreciated. We all like to know we count."
~ FRANCES COLE JONES, *How to Wow*

Acts 26:10b ~ ". . . but I also cast my vote . . ."

Deuteronomy 1:13 ESV ~ "Choose for your tribes wise, understanding, and experienced men, and I will appoint them as your heads."

Prayer
Lord of discernment,
As any election approaches, help us to educate ourselves on the issues and be able to make an informed decision. We have the ability to change the course of history with our one vote. Give us the nudge that's required. Amen.

Reflections from Week 12

1. The ways to make a difference I liked best this week were:

    ☐ Day 78　　☐ Day 81　　☐ Day 84
    ☐ Day 79　　☐ Day 82
    ☐ Day 80　　☐ Day 83

2. Did you supply a new mom and her family with dinner when she got home with the new baby? What was her response? How did you know her? Church, mutual organization, neighbor, friend, relative, or . . . ?

3. Did you connect with an old friend who lives out of your area? What did you talk about? What was their reaction? Did you both make plans to keep in touch?

4. Did Day 80 inspire you to clean your closets and donate items you no longer need or use? How did you feel after dropping the items off at the donation location? Are you inspired to do more sorting out of additional items for future donations?

5. When you smiled at a stranger, what was their response? Did you choose them randomly, or did you look in the faces of many before you made your choice?

6. In our communities, a project is always going on. Did you encourage someone to keep working? What was the project? Who was the person? What was their reaction?

7. Where did you shine your light this week? Who received your encouragement? How did that encouragement help?

8. In the last election, did you vote? Do you always vote or just sometimes? Do you encourage others to vote? How do you encourage them?

9. Were you inspired to do something additional to the seven items for this week and, if so, what did you do?

10. List some of the ways you felt while you were making a difference this week.

DO SOMETHING NICE FOR A STRANGER.

WHEN WAS THE last time you did something nice for a stranger? Although we were taught not to talk to strangers when we were young, our discernment of which strangers may be dangerous has improved with age. We have a lot of strangers to choose from out there.

You can choose a stranger in a store or a parking lot, on the road, in the airport, in a restaurant or a restroom, to name a few places. Just a smile can turn someone's day around. Have you ever thanked the person who cleans the restroom? This can be a thankless job, so a thank you makes a difference.

Being nice to a stranger can make their day, but it also has health benefits for us. Our heart rate goes down as well as our blood pressure. It gives us a sense of calmness, meaning, and purpose. All of this helps us live longer. Studies prove we are happier when we are kind, and people trust us more.[58] So be kind and make a difference.

"Too often we underestimate the power of a touch, a smile,
a kind word, a listening ear, or the smallest act of caring,
all of which have the potential to turn a life around."
~ LEO BUSCAGLIA (1924-1998)

"We must not, in trying to think about how we can make a big difference, ignore the small daily differences we can make which, over time, add up to big differences that we often cannot foresee."
~ MARIAN WRIGHT EDELMAN

Deuteronomy 10:18 ~ ". . . who executes justice for the orphan and the widow, and who loves the strangers, providing them food and clothing."

Matthew 25:35 ~ ". . . for I was hungry and you gave me food, I was thirsty and you gave me something to drink, I was a stranger and you welcomed me, . . ."

And don't forget the Good Samaritan in **Luke 10:30-37.**

Prayer
Loving Jesus,
As we go about our day, let us be kind to the person who may not get any kindness. Our smile, holding the door open for them, or a simple thank you for their help may encourage them to keep going. Thank You for the opportunity. Amen.

DAY 8 (86 overall): YOUR COUNTRY

PRAY FOR OTHERS IN NEED AND OUR COUNTRY.

THE WONDER OF prayer is that you can be petitioning on others' behalf, have an impact on their lives if it is God's will, and it opens your heart for the person or people in need. We see and read about a lot of misfortune around us—disease, disasters, violence, hunger, depression.... The need for prayer is growing every day. Think of the problems across the country. We are helpless to make much of a positive impact to correct those problems, but our prayers have strength through God. Praying for others increases our prayer life, expands our spiritual influence, and is therapeutic and rewarding for us.[59]

We might stew about something and then it finally hits us: *I will pray for the situation.* It's the best thing we can do and should have been the first thing we did. Prayer is always important and never a waste of time.

When I felt one of my customers at the Farmers' Market needed prayer, I stopped everything, asked them if we could pray together, held their hands, and we prayed. What we pray is not as important as that we pray. The Holy Spirit knows the desires of our heart.

Make a difference in someone else's life and pray for them. Pray for our country!

"Having a specific meaning and purpose in your life helps to encourage you towards living a fulfilling and inspired life."
~ VIC JOHNSON, *GOAL SETTING*

"Prayer is not overcoming God's reluctance, but laying hold of His willingness."
~ MARTIN LUTHER (1483-1546)

II Corinthians 1:11 ~ ". . . as you also join in helping us by your prayers, so that many will give thanks on our behalf for the blessing granted us through the prayers of many."

James 5:16 ~ "Therefore confess your sins to one another, and pray for one another, so that you may be healed. The prayer of the righteous is powerful and effective."

Prayer
Vigilant Lord,
As we pray for others, make us aware of their needs. Please accept our intercessory prayers and guide our language as we speak to You. Amen.

DAY 9 (87 overall): YOUR COUNTRY

PLANT A GARDEN, HELP BUILD A HOME WITH HABITAT FOR HUMANITY, OR VOLUNTEER WITH A DISASTER RELIEF PROJECT.

HABITAT FOR HUMANITY'S Frederick County, Maryland website states: "Habitat for Humanity is a nonprofit organization that helps families build and improve places to call home. We believe affordable housing plays a critical role in strong and stable communities."[60]

In 1969, the first Habitat for Humanity home was completed. Since then, over 13 million houses have been built or old homes made stronger. In 2007 and every year since, the annual Christmas Tree at Rockefeller Center, after being a focal point in the city, has been milled and that lumber donated to build a Habitat House.[61]

Through fundraising and volunteer help, Habitat for Humanity can continue its work. Examine your skills and they will find a place for you to use them. Whether it's helping with landscaping by planting shrubs, serving lunches for the workers, using a paint brush, or swinging a hammer, you are needed to make a difference in families' lives.

"We have the potential to help people out of poverty, out of disease, out of slavery, and out of conflict. Too often, we turn the other way because we think there's nothing we can do."
~ Alicia Keys

"There is no greater joy nor greater reward than to make a fundamental difference in someone's life."
~ Mary Rose McGeady

I Kings 5:5 ~ "So I intend to build a house for the name of the Lord my God, as the Lord said to my father David, 'Your son, whom I will set on your throne in your place, shall build the house for my name.'"

I Corinthians 3:10 ~ "According to the grace of God given to me, like a skilled master builder I laid a foundation, and someone else is building on it. Each builder must choose with care how to build on it."

Prayer
Generous God,
Thank You for our God-given skills. Help us use them to improve

others' situations by volunteering to use the talents You have given us. Encourage us to find those opportunities in our country. Amen.

PUT TOGETHER A PROGRAM TO TEACH OTHERS ABOUT CONSERVING OUR NATURAL RESOURCES.

THE UNITED STATES Department of Agriculture Natural Resources Conservation Service has programs that help people reduce soil erosion, enhance water supplies, improve water quality, increase wildlife habitat, and reduce damages caused by floods and other natural disasters. You could use these many programs to teach others about conservation.

HelpSaveNature.com states, "Natural resources are actually nature's gift to man to help him live a comfortable and peaceful life. But, at the same time, we as human beings have the responsibility of conserving natural resources by taking the right steps. This will help us maintain the environmental balance and satisfy our needs to the fullest. Importance of doing so can be conveyed to people by arranging seminars and conferences and having lectures of renowned environmental experts."[62]

You could present a program on water conservation. HelpSaveNature.com also notes, "Water is the most important resource, which should be conserved by adopting strict rules and measures. Often, we see wastage of water on a large-scale, which can be avoided by conducting training and information sessions to educate people. People should use minimum water for daily needs, such as washing cars and utensils. Whenever you see open taps, you should immediately go and close them properly to save water. The simple ways to save the environment will help you know more."[63]

You can begin at home and ripple out from there to make a difference.

"The conservation of natural resources is the fundamental
problem. Unless we solve that problem it will avail
us little to solve all others."
~ Theodore Roosevelt (1858-1919)

"The earth has enough resources for our need,
but not for our greed."
~ Mahatma Gandhi (1869-1948)

Job 12:7-10 ESV ~ "But ask the beasts, and they will teach you; the
birds of the heavens, and they will tell you; or the bushes of the earth,
and they will teach you; and the fish of the sea will declare to you.
Who among all these does not know that the hand of the Lord has
done this? In his hand is the life of every living thing and the breath
of all mankind."

Romans 15:14 ~ "I myself feel confident about you, my brothers
and sisters, that you yourselves are full of goodness, filled with all
knowledge, and able to instruct one another."

Prayer
God of all nature,
Guide us to protect the resources You have given us. Help us use
them wisely and conserve them for the generations to come. Encourage us to learn the best ways to protect them and to teach others
what we have learned. Amen.

DAY 11 (89 overall) ~ YOUR COUNTRY

BE POSITIVE WITH EACH PERSON YOU ENCOUNTER.

Just think what a country we would have if everyone thought
positively. True, some days this is easier than others, but we can
certainly strive for it.

Mayoclinic.org has information you might be interested in knowing: "It begins with positive thinking which helps with stress management and can even improve your health. Practice overcoming negative self-talk." Positive thinking just means that you approach unpleasantness in a more positive and productive way. You expect the best is going to happen, not the worst. If the thoughts that run through your head are mostly negative, your outlook on life is more likely pessimistic. If your thoughts are mostly positive, you're likely an optimist — someone who practices positive thinking.

Research continues on the effects that positive thinking and optimism have on health. However, health benefits of positive thinking may include the following:

- Increased life span
- Lower rates of depression
- Lower levels of distress
- Greater resistance to disease
- Better psychological and physical well-being
- Better cardiovascular health and reduced risk of death from cardiovascular disease
- Better coping skills when encountering hardships and times of stress[64]

"It's unclear why people who engage in positive thinking experience these health benefits. One theory is that having a positive outlook enables you to cope better with stressful situations, which reduces the harmful health effects of stress on your body. It's also thought that positive and optimistic people tend to live healthier lifestyles—they get more physical activity, follow a healthier diet, and don't smoke or drink alcohol in excess."[65]

When your state of mind is generally optimistic, you're better able to handle everyday stress in a more constructive way. That ability may contribute to the widely observed health benefits of positive thinking.

You can't go wrong being positive. It will make a positive difference!

"Having good days is a decision that we make every day before we even walk out the door."
~ Sumit Gautam

"The greater the difficulty, the more the glory in surmounting it."
~ Epicurus (341-270 BC)

1 Corinthians 13:4-7 ESV ~ "Love is patient and kind; love does not envy or boast; it is not arrogant or rude. It does not insist on its own way; it is not irritable or resentful; it does not rejoice at wrongdoing, but rejoices with the truth. Love bears all things, believes all things, hopes all things, endures all things."

Proverbs 31:26 ~ "She opens her mouth with wisdom, and the teaching of kindness is on her tongue."

Prayer
Positive Lord,
You have given us so many wonderful things for which to be grateful. Having a positive attitude and sharing that with others is what we will strive to do with Your help. Being optimistic does not mean we go around with rose-colored glasses. It means we look for the positive possibilities. Please help us be positive. Amen.

CHAPTER SIX

MAKE A DIFFERENCE IN YOUR WORLD

THIS CHAPTER IS about your farthest reaching influence. The ripples are farthest away from the initial spot where the rock was tossed, but the rock's impact still influences the ripples out here. God generated them to keep moving. Ride the ripples and continue to let Him influence your path so you can make a difference.

Why Make a Difference in Your World?

Six good reasons are to:

1. save a child;
2. feed a hungry family;
3. teach a community how to farm;
4. help a family raise livestock for food and make a living;
5. save the rain forests;
6. right social injustices.

DAY 1 (90 overall): YOUR WORLD

DO RESEARCH ON A CONTROVERSIAL TOPIC AND SHARE YOUR RESULTS WITH AN ORGANIZATION TO WHICH YOU BELONG.

Controversy keeps life interesting—just not too much of it. I avoid conflict as much as possible, but it's always good to look at a topic, do research on it, and share your findings with others. Your research could expand your current thinking, open your eyes to others' points of view, and give you a new perspective to think about. When you report your findings to the people of your organization, you could do the same for them—give them new information to consider. You may not change their minds, but you are helping them explore an alternate viewpoint.

"You are here to make a difference in this world, and the best way to do that is to use your knowledge and experience (on any topic, in any industry) to help others succeed."
~ Brendon Burchard, *The Millionaire Messenger*

". . . [I]t's imperative to discuss and explore issues (such as racism, sexism, immigration, etc.) inside the classroom so students feel empowered to speak up and take action outside the classroom."
~ Gabriella Corales

Acts 26:3 ~ ". . . because you are especially familiar with all the customs and controversies of the Jews; therefore I beg of you to listen to me patiently."

Titus 3:9 ~ "But avoid stupid controversies, genealogies, dissensions, and quarrels about the law, for they are unprofitable and worthless."

Prayer
Peaceful God,

As we do research on a topic of interest, help us look at both sides and come up with accurate results. May we not take offense at others with opposing views but learn from them and come to our own conclusions—those You would have us come to. Amen.

DAY 2 (91 overall): YOUR WORLD

RECYCLE IN WAYS YOU HADN'T THOUGHT OF DOING.

WE ALL KNOW how important recycling is! After we moved into our current house, when it was new over 30 years ago, we had monthly curbside heavy-item pickup. On the day before the pickup, with our heavy items out by the curb, a person came by in a truck and was looking through our items. My sixth-grade daughter opened the door and yelled at him, telling him to leave. I closed the door and sent her on her way. I waited for an hour or so to pass and then used this as a teaching moment. I asked her if she believed in recycling.

She said, "Oh yes. Recycling is important. It keeps things out of the landfill."

My response was, "What do you think that man was doing? He was going to reuse the items he put in his truck and keep them from going in the landfill." My statement gave her something to ponder and the look on her face showed just that.

Recycling matters for many reasons:

1. **It's good for our economy.** American companies rely on recycling programs to provide the raw materials they need to make new products.
2. **It creates jobs.** Recycling in the U.S. is a $236 billion-a-year industry. More than 56,000 recycling and reuse enterprises use 1.1 million workers nationwide.
3. **It reduces waste.** The average American discards seven and a half pounds of garbage every day. Most of this garbage goes into landfills, where it's compacted and buried.

4. **It's good for the environment.** Using recycled materials for manufacturing requires far less energy and uses fewer natural resources than using raw materials. It also keeps waste from piling up in landfills.

5. **It saves energy.** Recycling offers significant energy savings over manufacturing with virgin materials. Manufacturing with recycled aluminum cans uses 95 percent less energy than using virgin aluminum.

6. **It preserves landfill space.** No one wants to live next door to a landfill. Recycling preserves existing landfill space.

7. **It prevents global warming.** In 2000, recycling of solid waste prevented the release of 32.9 million metric tons of carbon equivalent (MMTCE, the unit of measure for greenhouse gases) into the air.

8. **It reduces water pollution.** Making goods from recycled materials generates far less water pollution than manufacturing from virgin materials.

9. **It protects wildlife.** Using recycled materials reduces the need to damage forests, wetlands, rivers, and other places essential to wildlife.

10. **It creates new demand.** Recycling and buying recycled products create demand for more recycled products, decreasing waste and helping our economy.[66]

Let's look at interesting ways you can recycle by reusing various items.

1. Reuse plastic bottles for craft items, to store snack foods, as planters, as pet food or bird seed scoops, as toys, etc. (For more ideas go to: *www.budgetdumpster.com/blog/ diy-plastic-bottles-recycling/*.)

2. Reuse coffee filters. Rinse out grounds and the filters are already dyed a natural color. Or use them in the bottom of plant pots so dirt doesn't escape from the drainage hole but water will. (More ideas: *diyinspired.com/ recycled-coffee-filter-inspiration/*)

3. Use old bicycle parts or plastic bottles to make chande-
    liers. Use old pallets to make a vertical planter or tiered
    seating for a home theater. (For photos of fascinating,
    often beautiful, creative ideas: *www.boredpanda.com/
    awesome-recycling-ideas/*)

If you **reduce, reuse, recycle**, you can make a difference in the
world.

My basil wall using old pallets and gutters

"If it can't be reduced, reused, repaired, rebuilt, refurbished,
refinished, resold, recycled, or composted, then it should be
restricted, redesigned or removed from production."
~ PETE SEEGER (1919-2014), FOLK SINGER AND SOCIAL ACTIVIST

"We are living on this planet as if we had another one to go to."
~ TERRY SWEARINGEN, NURSE AND WINNER OF GOLDMAN
ENVIRONMENTAL PRIZE IN 1997

Proverbs 3:19 ~ "The Lord by wisdom founded the earth; by understanding he established the heavens; . . ."

Genesis 1:31 ESV ~ "And God saw everything that he had made, and behold, it was very good."

Prayer
Resourceful God,
Help us keep our landfills free of reusable items. Teach us to be creative and come up with ideas of how we can reuse items, making them into useful treasures. Amen.

DAY 3 (92 overall): YOUR WORLD

PRAY FOR OTHERS IN CRISIS.

I HAVE GIVEN you many reasons why prayer is important, but praying for people in crisis throughout the world can be lifesaving. Many crises are ravaging the world:

1. "Around the world, as many as 811 million people regularly go to bed hungry."[67]
2. South Korea and China have a birth crisis. Not enough couples are having babies, so the population is decreasing drastically. China now allows three babies per couple.[68]
3. Venezuela has a health care crisis. "The country's health system is collapsing. Hospitals have closed or are operating at a fraction of their capacity, many without regular access to electricity or water."[69]
4. China has a food crisis.[70]
5. Depression, mental health issues caused by COVID-19, senior citizens living in poverty, financial problems, and more are all contributing to a suicide crisis.[71]
6. Violence, disease, and malnutrition are prevalent throughout Africa and the Middle East, and even in the United States.[72]
7. Lack of safe drinking water in many places is causing health crises.[73]
8. Human trafficking is increasing around the world.[74]

9. The COVID-19 pandemic has caused many deaths and much misery.

These are sobering facts. Since God is in charge, praying is a necessity. We can't fix everything, but He can. If He inspires you to do more than pray (which is powerful in itself), follow His lead and you could make even more of a difference!

> "Everything you do and every decision you make should be from a place of good. You should always be striving to make the world a better place."
> ~ LES BROWN, *LAWS OF SUCCESS*

> "And all I'm saying is, see, what a wonderful world it would be if only we'd give it a chance. Love, baby, love. That's the secret, yeah. If lots more of us loved each other, we'd solve lots more problems."
> ~ LOUIS ARMSTRONG (1901-1971)

Proverbs 3:5-6 ~ "Trust in the LORD with all your heart, and do not rely on your own insight. In all your ways acknowledge him, and he will make straight your paths."

Matthew 19:26 ~ "But Jesus looked at them and said, 'For mortals it is impossible, but for God all things are possible.'"

Prayer
Inspiring Jesus,
You helped people in crisis all through the Bible. Guide us now to help people in crisis with our prayers. Inspire us to do more with our prayers and go outside of our own country and work to help where we can. Remind us that our situation is not so bad in comparison. Amen.

Reflections from Week 13 + 1 Day

1. The ways to make a difference I liked best this week were:

    ☐ Day 85   ☐ Day 88   ☐ Day 91
    ☐ Day 86   ☐ Day 89   ☐ Day 92
    ☐ Day 87   ☐ Day 90

2. What nice thing did you do for a stranger? Where were you? How did they react?
3. What person or people in need did you pray for? What was their need?
4. When did you volunteer for Habitat for Humanity or work for a disaster relief project? Where did you go? What did you do? Would you do it again?
5. Where did you get the information for your conservation project? With which group did you share the information? How was it received?
6. What positive thing did you do with the people you encountered? Where were you? What was their reaction?
7. What controversial topic did you choose? Where did you get your information? To whom did you present it? Was there a lot of discussion?
8. What new ways did you reduce, recycle, and/or reuse this week? Where did you get the ideas for this new project?
9. What crisis did you pray for, and what did your prayer include? Did you feel better afterwards?
10. Were you inspired to do something additional to the eight items for this week and, if so, what did you do?
11. List some of the ways you felt while you were making a difference this week.

SHARE THE GOSPEL WITH SOMEONE.

SHARING THE GOSPEL may not be easy for us, but Jesus commanded us in Mark 16:15 to preach the gospel throughout the world to every creature. From this directive, we can count on the Lord to equip us with the tools we need to share. Loving our neighbors as much as we love ourselves gives us even more reason to share the gospel. As believers, we feel thankful to the person who shared the gospel with us, and we should express that gratitude by sharing it with others.

Pastor Rick Warren gives us 10 reasons to share the gospel:

1. God made us to know Him.
2. Evangelism was Jesus' mission—and we're called to do likewise.
3. Evangelism is our responsibility.
4. Evangelism is a privilege.
5. Evangelism shows your gratitude for what Jesus has done for you.
6. People are hopelessly lost without Christ.
7. God wants everyone saved.
8. You'll be rewarded for eternity.
9. God's timetable for history hinges on us completing our mission.
10. We'll be glad when we see people in heaven.[75]

The gospel gives us hope and increases our joy, so make a difference and share it with others.

"So, no matter what your age, keep yourself motivated by setting goals. By being active, by making a difference in others' lives. Don't think once you reach a certain age you can stop. Or don't let your age make you feel that you have all the time in the world. None of us are guaranteed tomorrow. Make a difference today."

~ CATHERINE PULSIFER

"To be a star, you must shine your own light, follow your path, and don't worry about the darkness, for that is when the stars shine brightest. Always do what you are afraid to do."
~ Ralph Waldo Emerson (1803-1882)

Mark 16:15 ~ "And he said to them, 'Go into all the world and proclaim the good news to the whole creation.'"

I Thessalonians 2:8 ~ "So deeply do we care for you that we are determined to share with you not only the gospel of God but also our own selves, because you have become very dear to us."

Prayer
Faithful Jesus,
Give us the courage, the tools, and the opportunity to share the gospel throughout the world. We may not be the one traveling, but we can support the people who *are* with prayer and financial aid. Remind us to pray for the missionaries and their work as well as the oppressed, that they will be able to worship despite their oppression. Amen.

DAY 5 (94 overall): YOUR WORLD

ADOPT A CHILD, A PET, OR A PLANT.

To adopt is a very personal decision, whether you adopt a child, a pet, or a plant. People have many reasons to adopt a child. Here are five:

1. You can give a child a better life than they currently have (living in foster care, living with someone who cannot take care of them, living in a foreign country but not thriving there, etc.).
2. You can still raise a child even if you can't give birth for medical reasons.
3. You can save a child from being aborted.

4. You feel called to adopt for religious reasons.
5. You were adopted and want to give another child the same love and opportunities you had.

Reasons to adopt a pet:

1. You can save an animal from homelessness, as the shelters are full.
2. You want a pet but one that's already housebroken.
3. The animal is already spayed or neutered, which saves you the expense.
4. You want to save an animal from euthanasia.
5. You can decide the age of your pet and miss the mischievous puppy or kitten stage if you choose.

If adopting a child or pet is not for you, a plant is a good alternative because a plant . . .

1. doesn't need a babysitter;
2. doesn't need to be taken outside to walk or relieve itself;
3. can fulfill a need but requires little care;
4. helps clean your environment—taking in carbon dioxide and producing oxygen;
5. adds beauty to your space;
6. may be useful, such as herbs you can eat or aloe vera you can use for skin care and healing.

"To adopt a child is a great work of love. When it is done, much is given, but much is also received. It is a true exchange of gifts."
~ POPE JOHN PAUL II (1920-2005)

"Over the years I have felt the truest, purest love—
the love of God, really, I imagine that's what God's love
feels like—is the love that comes from your dog."
~ OPRAH WINFREY

Acts 7:21 ~ ". . . and when he was abandoned, Pharaoh's daughter adopted him and brought him up as her own son."

Ephesians 1:5 ~ "He destined us for adoption as his children through Jesus Christ, according to the good pleasure of his will, . . ."

Prayer
Father of us all,
Thank you for adopting us into Your family so we can be in heaven with You for eternity. Help us share that love on earth with children, animals, and/or plants. Amen.

DAY 6 (95 overall): YOUR WORLD

EXPLORE WAYS TO VOLUNTEER VIRTUALLY.

You can help fulfill the great need for volunteers right from home on your computer.

Kelly Corbett from *House Beautiful* did an article on this in April 2020[76] and gives us nine ways you can volunteer virtually. I've added one more for a list of 10:

1. **Be a listening ear** for someone struggling right now. Get trained to volunteer on a Crisis Help Line. (Search Crisis Helpline Volunteer for opportunities with various organizations.)
2. **Find a volunteer opportunity tailored to your skills and interests.** Do you have skills to design a brochure or translate information into another language, or do you have another skillset that might be useful to a nonprofit? Check out CATCHFIRE! Ministries, a platform where nonprofits post open volunteer opportunities. *(www.catchfire.org)*
3. **Answer questions about your job** from students/future entrepreneurs who want to learn more about what you do. *(https://www.score.org/volunteer)*

4. **Sew blankets for BINKY PATROL.** These blankets are donated to hospitals or shelters. *(https://binkypatrol.org/)*

5. **Help out kids with reading barriers.** BookShare is an e-book library that helps people with dyslexia, learning disabilities, visual impairments, physical disabilities, and other reading barriers to read and enjoy stories. Containing over 800,000 titles, BookShare is always looking for volunteers to help expand its library. Volunteers can scan books to the platform, as well as proofread and describe images. *(https://www.bookshare.org/cms/)*

6. **Join the United Nations Volunteer Force.** Each year, over 12,000 volunteers from 187 countries help the United Nation further its mission of spreading peace and development worldwide—all from their computers. Volunteers can choose from a range of tasks such as writing and editing, art and design, research, event planning, and more. *(https://www.unv.org/tags/un-online-volunteers)*

7. **Virtually walk for cancer.** If you've ever participated in an American Cancer Society Relay for Life event, you're familiar with how the community-wide fundraising event operates. Now, instead of camping out and walking for loved ones in real life, you can do it in a virtual world. *https://www.cancer.org/involved/volunteer/virtual.html)*

8. **Become an online tutor.** The program **Learn to Be** offers free and low-cost one-on-one tutoring sessions to students from kindergarten to 12th grade. You can apply to become a tutor and help students with their five-paragraph essays, math homework, and more during one-hour virtual sessions. The program even accepts high school volunteers. *(https://www.learntobe.org/)*

9. **Post on social media for a good cause through the American Red Cross.** If you're social-media-savvy, you might enjoy partaking in American Red Cross's digital volunteer opportunities. Volunteers can help out just by sharing important disaster updates and resources on their personal social media accounts. Furthermore, volunteers may

be asked to monitor online conversations with disaster-affected people, as well as serving as a compassionate voice to those impacted. Another way to help (although it's non-virtual), is by donating blood to the American Red Cross. There has been a massive decline in donations during the pandemic as blood drives across the country have been cancelled. *(www.redcross.org)*

10. **Lend your eyes.** Another idea from **Be My Eyes** is to lend your eyes to solve tasks big and small to help blind and low-vision people lead more independent lives. Whenever a blind or low-vision person needs visual assistance, volunteers are happy to help. Through a live video call on a free mobile phone app, they and a volunteer can communicate directly and solve a problem. The volunteer will help guide which direction to point the person's camera or where to focus.

    As a sighted volunteer, you can help by first installing the Be My Eyes app. A blind or low-vision user may need help with anything from checking expiration dates, distinguishing colors, reading instructions, or navigating new surroundings. These tasks can be done through a video phone call. *(bemyeyes.com)*

Are you drawn to help in any of these capacities? Any or all of these volunteer jobs make a difference!

"The purpose of life is not to be happy. It is to be useful,
to be honorable, to be compassionate, to have it make
some difference that you have lived and lived well."
~ Ralph Waldo Emerson (1803-1882)

"The older I get, the greater power
I seem to have to help the world."
~ Susan B. Anthony (1820-1906)

I Chronicles 28:21b ~ ". . . and with you in all the work will be every volunteer who has skill for any kind of service; . . ."

Acts 20:35 ~ "In all this I have given you an example that by such work we must support the weak, remembering the words of the Lord Jesus, for he himself said, 'It is more blessed to give than to receive.'"

Prayer
Assisting God,
Let us follow Your example by giving of ourselves to others who need help but cannot afford to pay anyone. Help us realize that as volunteers we get as much or more out of the experience than do the people we help. Encourage us to get out there and make a difference. Amen.

DAY 7 (96 overall): YOUR WORLD

GIVE A SMALL MONETARY DONATION. (IF 1,000 PEOPLE GIVE $.50, THAT WOULD EQUAL $500.)

AS WE HAVE heard many times, "Every penny counts." Small donations from many people can have a big impact when they're combined and can make a big difference to the recipients. For example, elementary students may pool their change to donate to a worthy cause; people drop change and dollars into the Salvation Army bell ringers' buckets that are returned to the community to do good; and on a larger scale, United Way donations go to support local nonprofits that help others. Every donation truly makes a difference.

Following are reasons to give, even if the dollar amount seems small:

1. Most nonprofits, no matter their size, need all the help they can get.

2. Small donations add up.
3. It's not the size of the contribution that matters; it's the outcome your giving produces.
4. Regardless of the amount you can contribute, the heart of the donor (you!) is what counts.

Not only will you make a difference in the lives of others, but your life will also be changed for the better.

At church, we have a "noisy" offering one Sunday a month, collecting change or "not-so-noisy" paper money. We are a small congregation, but that change adds up, and the designated recipient is happy for whatever the donation is.

Everyone's change adds up to make a difference

Regardless of the amount, most giving requires some level of sacrifice on the donor's part. Collectively, all our donations impact our community, our country, and the world. So be proud of the difference you and your family can make.

"It's not how much we give,
but how much love we put into giving."
~ Mother Teresa (1910-1997)

"Little by little, a little becomes A LOT."
~ Tanzanian proverb

Luke 21:1-4 ESV ~ "Jesus looked up and saw the rich putting their gifts into the offering box, and he saw a poor widow put in two small copper coins. And he said, 'Truly, I tell you, this poor widow has put in more than all of them. For they all contributed out of their abundance, but she out of her poverty put in all she had to live on.'"

Luke 6:38 ESV ~ "Give, and it will be given to you. Good measure, pressed down, shaken together, running over, will be put into your lap. For with the measure you use it will be measured back to you."

Prayer
Ever-giving Savior,
Thank You for Your generous gift. You have given us everything we have. Let us reciprocate by giving what we can to worthwhile organizations. Amen.

DAY 8 (97 overall): YOUR WORLD

TAKE A MISSION TRIP.

SOME OF YOU may have gone on a mission trip for several reasons. Jamie Booth wrote, "I love mission trips. They give people the opportunity to make a huge impact on their world, and they also give the world the opportunity to impact the people that go on them. Some of the most memorable, and formative, moments of my life have been on mission trips. There are just so many reasons for people to go on a short-term mission trip."[77]

My sister Sandy and her husband Christ went on three mission trips to Pineridge Native American Reservation in South Dakota. As a master gardener, she brought soil and plants. Some of the plants were from her garden and some plants and pots had been donated at a reduced price by the University of Wisconsin at River Falls. Her husband brought boards and the tools needed to make raised beds. Their truck and the trailer with the church logo on the side that they pulled behind was full to the brim. On the way, their truck began to malfunction. They stopped at a Ford dealership and the person who made the minor repair didn't charge them anything because of where they were going and what they were going to do once they got there. He told them it was an early Christmas present—very early because it was May. They were on their way to do something significant.

The people on the reservation were "delightful" and very welcoming. They appreciated all Sandy and her husband did for them. Sandy said she learned to be grateful with no complaining, for these people had next to nothing, without much chance of the situation changing. She was grateful to play a part in making these people's lives a little better.

I have a friend who goes to Guatemala several times every year, doing different things—whatever is needed. Sometimes she teaches, and sometimes she helps her brother, who works with Doctors Without Borders. On her latest trip, she helped her brother's church team install almost 100 vented stoves in a week. The new stoves, made of 11 cement blocks, replaced open fires that were hazards children could fall into and not vented to the outside so the residents were breathing in the smoke all day long. The new ones solved both problems: They were enclosed, making them safer for children, and they were vented to the outside so their homes were smoke free. One additional benefit: If the people moved, they could disassemble their stove and take it with them. My friend felt grateful to be a part of this project and make a difference in each family's life.

On a mission trip, *you* could make a difference in the world through people's lives.

"When ordinary people decide to step out and be part of something big, that's when they become extraordinary."
~ Brett Harris, *Do Hard Things*

"Grant me courage to serve others; for in service there is true life."
~ Cesar Chavez (1927-1993)

Judges 18:6 ~ "The priest replied, 'Go in peace. The mission you are on is under the eye of the Lord.'"

Mark 6:6 ~ "Then he went about among the villages teaching."

Prayer
Self-sacrificing Jesus,
Thank You for Your example of helping others. A mission trip is an outstanding way for us to fulfill this. Please touch our hearts with the desire to go on a mission trip, doing what we can to help others. Amen.

DAY 9 (98 overall): YOUR WORLD

SUPPORT A CHILD IN ANOTHER COUNTRY.

MY OLDEST DAUGHTER Sabrina and her husband Eric have been sponsoring children since before they were even married. They were led to do this for many reasons. When he was still her boyfriend, not yet her husband, he gave a sponsorship to her as one of his very first gifts. The cost was only $1.00 a day for each child. That money provided educational opportunities, food, clothing, and access to clean water. Some special gifts during the years were mosquito netting, farm animals, special outfits for festivals, and extra money for a special medical procedure. Their generosity helped with whatever the sponsored community needed. For example, they helped the family of their sponsored children obtain adequate housing.

This kind of donation gives hope to the families because they know someone cares about them and contributes to a better life for them.

My daughter chose a child with the closest birthdate to her children's, and the children write to each other periodically. My grandchildren pray for these children in another country every night. This helps them grow up with compassion and learn about people in other circumstances than theirs. My daughter's family knows they can't help every child, but they do what they can.

The experience of sponsoring has been a very important part of all their lives, changing one life at a time in the world.

You could make a big difference in a child's life.

"One must not focus on the risk of saying, 'Yes.' The greater risk is missing opportunities by saying, 'No.'"
~ Charles Sullivan, *Never Say Never, Never Say No*

"I'd rather regret the things I have done than the things that I haven't."
~ Lucille Ball (1911-1989)

Luke 18:15-17 ~ "People were bringing even infants to him that he might touch them; and when the disciples saw it, they sternly ordered them not to do it. But Jesus called for them and said, 'Let the little children come to me, and do not stop them; for it is to such as these that the kingdom of God belongs. Truly I tell you, whoever does not receive the kingdom of God as a little child will never enter it.'"

Matthew 25:40 ~ "And the king will answer them, 'Truly I tell you, just as you did it to one of the least of these who are members of my family, you did it to me.'"

Prayer
Heavenly Father,
You watch out for all Your children. Spark the desire in our hearts to help a child with our donations. With our money, we can change a child's life forever with proper nutrition, an education, and opportunities they can't even dream of. Help us fulfill this need. Amen.

DAY 10 (99 overall): YOUR WORLD

KEEP A GRATITUDE JOURNAL. CHOOSE ONE OF THE 100 ITEMS YOU ARE MOST THANKFUL FOR AND FIND A WAY TO SPREAD IT AROUND THE WORLD.

THERE ARE MANY reasons to keep a gratitude journal. Focusing on the positive things that happen on a given day is better than focusing on the negative. Arianna Huffington, author of *Thrive,* notes, "Gratitude works its magic by serving as an antidote to negative emotions. It's like white blood cells for the soul, protecting us from cynicism, entitlement, anger, and resignation."[78]

Do your best to write in your journal every night before going to sleep. Keep it on your nightstand or side table next to your bed. It will be close and remind you. You don't have to spend a lot of time, maybe 5 or 10 minutes, but this practice helps you focus on the positive things in your life. See if you can write down between 5 and 10 items each night. They don't have to be detailed, although they can be, but just being grateful for the sunshine, the full moon, or family can be enough. When you find time to write, the benefits are worth it.

Keeping a gratitude journal:

1.   Improves physical health by improving heart rate and blood pressure. It helps control blood sugar levels and reduces complaints about how you feel.

2. Improves your mental well-being. By being grateful the stresses of life can be dealt with more positively.
3. Promotes spiritual growth. You may begin to trust that you are divinely guided if you have faith and trust your guidance.
4. Increases self-esteem. By appreciating your daily blessings, the things you don't have become less important.
5. Reduces stress, which can put you in a stable state of calm despite outside demands.
6. Helps you sleep better, especially if you write in your gratitude journal before falling asleep. You focus on the good in your life instead of the things pressing in on you.
7. Improves your relationships, because if you feel better about yourself, you can focus on others, and they will feel better about themselves, knowing you care.[79]

On days when you feel down, read back through your gratitude journal to readjust your attitude and remember that you have many blessings in your life.

After you have written in your journal for several months, reread it, choose the item you are most thankful for, and post it on social media to send it around the world.

"As we express our gratitude, we must never forget that the highest appreciation is not to utter words, but to live by them."
~ JOHN F. KENNEDY (1917-1963)

"Let gratitude be the pillow upon which you
kneel to say your nightly prayer."
~ MAYA ANGELOU (1928-2014)

Ephesians 5:20 ~ ". . . giving thanks to God the Father at all times and for everything in the name of our Lord Jesus Christ."

1 Thessalonians 5:18 ~ ". . . [G]ive thanks in all circumstances; for this is the will of God in Christ Jesus for you."

Prayer
Precious Savior,
Spark a grateful spirit within us. We have so much to be thankful for because of You. As we write down our blessings, let us reflect on them and tell the people we are grateful for what they mean to us. Amen.

DAY 11 (100 overall ~ OUR LAST DAY): YOUR WORLD

THINK ABOUT THE PEOPLE IN YOUR LIFE THAT MADE A DIFFERENCE IN YOU.

This is the last day of our 100-day journey. Thank you for reading and for your involvement in making a difference—whatever you chose to do. This day requires some thinking on your part. Think about the people in your life that made a difference in who you are today and who you want to become. They could be your parents, other family members, friends, neighbors, teachers, pastors, or others. As the ripples move out, the people on the outer ripples can have influence on you as well. If you can, write a letter or call some of the people who made a difference in you and let them know. It could make a difference to them just knowing they made a difference in you!

This photo is of my friend Irene. She is my biggest supporter, my cheerleader, and always there with a helping hand. She has made and still does make a difference in my life.

My friend Irene, who has been one of my biggest supporters, encouragers, and cheerleaders

This entire 100-day journey to make a difference idea came from my friend Marcia Doring. When asked who made a difference in her life, she said "Donna." I thought she meant some other Donna, but she meant me! I was shocked. I thought back over the years and didn't really know why I was the one she named.

My purpose in telling you this story is we don't know what kind of influence we have on others, but what we do and who we are *does* make a difference.

> "When I look back upon my early days I am stirred by the
> thought of the number of people whom I have to thank
> for what they gave me or for what they were to me."
> ~ Albert Schweitzer (1875-1965)

"When we get to the end of our life, the question playing over and over in our mind will be, 'Did my life make a difference?'"
~ Brian Fleming, *Your Life Matters*

I Chronicles 12:17a ~ "David went out to meet them and said to them, 'If you have come to me in friendship, to help me, then my heart will be knit to you; . . .'"

Mark 12:28-31 ESV ~ "'Which commandment is the most important of all?' Jesus answered, 'The most important is, Hear, O Israel: The Lord our God, the Lord is one. And you shall love the Lord your God with all your heart and with all your soul and with all your mind and with all your strength. The second is this: You shall love your neighbor as yourself. There is no other commandment greater than these.'"

Prayer
Thank You, God, for all the people You put in my life. You put each there for a purpose, and I am grateful You did. They have made all the difference in my life. And thank You for the blessings You have bestowed on me. Amen.

Reflections from Week 14 + 1 Day

1. The ways to make a difference I liked best this week were:

☐ Day 93   ☐ Day 96   ☐ Day 99
☐ Day 94   ☐ Day 97   ☐ Day 100
☐ Day 95   ☐ Day 98

2. Do you feel nervous about sharing the gospel? Did you share it anyway? What was the response?
3. This week did you adopt a child, pet, or plant, and if yes, from where? How is it working out?
4. Did you explore ways to volunteer virtually? What did you find? What was your favorite? Did you follow through and contact the organization?
5. Did you donate some money for a good cause? What place did you support?
6. Have you ever gone on a mission trip? Do you have plans to go again? What stood out the most in your mind from the experience?
7. Have you ever sponsored a child in another country? Would you consider sponsoring a child—or more than one? What is stopping you?
8. Do you own a gratitude journal? If not, will you purchase or create one? How often do you write in your journal? What benefit do you receive from writing in your gratitude journal?
9. Make a list of all the people who have made a difference in your life. Who has had the most influence? What did they do that made so much difference?
10. Were you inspired to do something additional to the eight items for this week and, if so, what did you do?
11. List some of the ways you felt while you were making a difference this week.

CONCLUSION

YOU CAN SEE that as the ripples move outward, there is always something that can be done to make a difference, so hop on board and do what you can. Remember, at times another person's ripples will blend with yours—and working together is even better.

Ask yourself:

1. Was there an experience in my life that changed me?
2. Have I let go of some things so I can find peace?
3. When did I live out the Love of Christ today?
4. Did I use my talents to bless others?
5. Did I help those overlooked or unnoticed by the world?
6. Will I leave the world a better place than I found it?
7. How am I trying to see more of God and less of myself in the world?
8. Who is writing my life story? God would like to.
9. Have I seen Jesus show up in unexpected ways?

The following story posted on Kindspring.org makes an important point we need to remember.

A man was asked to paint a boat. He brought his paint and brushes and began to paint the boat a bright red, as the owner asked him. While painting, he noticed a small hole in the hull, and quietly repaired it. When he finished painting, he received his money and left.

The next day, the owner of the boat came to the painter and presented him with a nice check, much higher

209

than the payment for painting. The painter was surprised and said, "You've already paid me for painting the boat, sir!"

"But this is not for the paint job. It's for repairing the hole in the boat."

"Ah! But it was such a small service . . . certainly it's not worth paying me such a high amount for something so insignificant."

"My dear friend, you do not understand. Let me tell you what happened: When I asked you to paint the boat, I forgot to mention the hole. When the boat dried, my kids took the boat and went on a fishing trip. They did not know that there was a hole. I was not at home at that time. When I returned and noticed they had taken the boat, I was desperate because I remembered that the boat had a hole. Imagine my relief and joy when I saw them returning from fishing. Then, I examined the boat and found that you had repaired the hole!

"You see, now, what you did? You saved the life of my children! I do not have enough money to pay your 'small' good deed."

Moral of the story: So, no matter who, when or how, just continue to help, sustain, wipe tears, listen attentively and carefully repair all the "leaks" you find, because you never know when one is in need of us or when God holds a pleasant surprise for us to be helpful and important to someone.[80]

Along the way, you may have repaired numerous "boat holes" without realizing how many lives you've saved.

God will never let go of our hand. He is limited only by our lack of faith. So, step out in faith and the barriers will be eliminated.

"Not until you believe one person can make a difference will you be willing to take a risk. Quit being so careful about protecting your own back. Stop worrying about what others will think. You

don't answer to them. You answer to Him. He will help. He will give you wisdom and courage. You may be only one, but you are one. So, take a risk!"[81]
~ CHARLES SWINDOLL

II Timothy 4:7 ~ "I have fought the good fight, I have finished the race, I have kept the faith."

II Corinthians 13:11 ~ "Finally, brothers and sisters, farewell. Put things in order, listen to my appeal, agree with one another, live in peace; and the God of love and peace will be with you."

ADDITIONAL IDEAS

ON THE DAYS that I gave you an idea that wasn't right for you, look at the ideas below and consider substituting one of these for the original idea.

1. In times of trouble, list and be thankful for your blessings and help others do the same.
2. Pick up and dispose of any trash you find on the side of the road in your neighborhood.
3. Visit or call an elderly friend or relative who doesn't get out much just to have a chat.
4. Take a moment and silently send love to the whole world and its inhabitants.
5. Take a walk with a small child and see the world through his or her eyes.
6. Hug someone (with their permission) who needs a little love.
7. Pray for God's highest good for your friends and family.
8. Pray for peace within yourself and peace in the world.
9. Have a family game night.
10. Write down five hopeful statements or positive affirmations, read them often, and if you're so inspired, share them with friends or post them on social media.
11. Raise your spirits and thus the spirits of those around you by dancing as if no one is watching and spending time looking at stars on a cloudless night and marveling at the majesty of the universe.

Search on Facebook for "Random Acts of Kristen" and follow examples posted by others. (Kristen was a beautiful young woman who died of breast cancer. Her family and friends established this page to honor her memory and share what a wonderful person she was.)

ABOUT THE AUTHOR

Donna Frawley WAS born in Minnesota and became a Home Economics teacher, which shouldn't surprise readers of this book. In 1977, she moved to Midland, Michigan. For 40 years now, she has owned and run Frawley's Fine Herbary *(frawleysfineherbary. com)*, which offers 60 different culinary mixes, herbal teas, and gift boxes.

Donna loves to write about her passions. She has written a monthly article for the *Midland Daily News* since 2002 and a monthly article for *Midland Neighbors* magazine since December of 2019. She has also published the weekly online newsletter *Cooking with Herbs* since January 2018. In addition, Donna is the author of *The Herbal Breads Cookbook* and *Our Favorite Recipes*, which are available on her website. She has developed a passion for writing fiction and nonfiction, with an historical fiction book in the works and the debut of this nonfiction book, *100 Ways to Make a Difference*.

One of Donna's passions is living according to the teachings of the Lord Jesus and being as helpful to others as she can. In this faith-based book, she presents ways to be a positive influence in other people's lives and leave a legacy of love. Others say, "She's been doing this her whole life!"

Donna's been married to Nile, her high school sweetheart, for 50 years. They have three married daughters, Sabrina, Samantha, and Veronica, and 10 grandchildren, with number 11 on the way. They all touch her heart in unique ways and make a wonderful difference in her life.

ENDNOTES

Introduction

1   Penny L. Howe, March 20, 2013, "The Ripple effect – How to succeed in life!" Retrieved in June 2020 from *https://thewhyaboutthis.com/2013/03/20/the-ripple-effect-how-to-succeed-in-life/*.

2   All scripture quotations are taken from the New Revised Standard Version (NRSV) of the Holy Bible unless otherwise attributed to the English Standard Version (ESV).

3   Reverend James Smith, from his Sunday sermon on November 15, 2020, Trinity and St. John's churches in Three Rivers, Michigan.

4   Holy Father Pope Francis, April 3, 2020. Busselton Catholic Parish. Retrieved in August 2020 from https://www.sjparish.org.au/post/pope-francis-river-do-not-drink.

Chapter 1: Make a Difference in Yourself

5   Lucy Larcom, "Plant a Tree." Retrieved in January 2021 from https://artsandcraftspress.com/blogs/news/64762693-plant-a-tree-by-lucy-larcom.

6   Loren Eiseley, "The Starfish Story." Excerpted from a 16-page essay called "The Star Thrower," in Eiseley's The Unexpected Universe, Harcourt, Brace & World, 1969, and Harper Collins, 1972.

7   Sanam Hafeez (n.d.). Retrieved in May 2020 from https://lazarev-international.com/news/world/how-to-get-better-at-admitting-youre-wrong/.

8   Wendy Rose Gould, NBC News. Retrieved in March 2022 from https://lazarev-international.com/news/world/how-to-get-better-at-admitting-youre-wrong/.

9   Ibid.

10   Darius Graham, Being the Difference: True Stories of Ordinary People Doing Extraordinary Things to Change the World. Charleston, South Carolina: BookSurge Publishing, 2007.

11   Linda Canup, "14 Benefits of Prayer – Saving Yourself Headache and Heartache," May 18, 2015. Retrieved in June 2020 from https://www.intouch.org.

12   Som Bathla (The Mindset Makeover), January 26, 2018. Retrieved in May 2020 from https://www.wow4u.com/makingadifference/.

13   Rebecca Joy Stanborough, November 10, 2020. Retrieved in November 2020 from https://www.healthline.com/health/benefits-of-singing.

14   Jung Shim (n.d.). Retrieved in June 2020 from https://www.jungshim.org/energy-blog/symptoms/6-reasons-take-walk-nature. (This link has been redirected to sunkyeong.org.)

15   Sarah of "How Wee Learn." Nature (n.d.). Retrieved in June 2020 from https://www.howweelearn.com/.

16   Amanda Hernandez, May 30, 2018. Retrieved in June 2020 from https://feedtosucceed.com.

17   Catherine Winter (n.d.). Retrieved in June 2020 from https://www.lifehack.org.

18   Corina Semph (n.d.). Retrieved in June 2020 from https://tinybuddha.com/blog.

19   Erma Bombeck (n.d.). Retrieved in June 2020 from https://www.goodreads.com/quotes.

Chapter 2: Make a Difference in Your Family
20   Sophie Martin, June 20, 2013. Retrieved in July 2020 from https://thoughtcatalog.com.

21   Babymommytime (n.d.), "12 Amazing Benefits of Grandparents in our Children's Lives." Retrieved in June 2020 from https://babymommytime.com/grandparents-family-childrens/.

22   Lisa Esposito, September 13, 2017. The Health Benefits of Having (and Being) Grandparents. Retrieved in June 2020 from https://health.usnews.com/wellness.

23   Lidiya Kesarovska, January 22, 2020. "How Listening to Others Can Make You a Better Person." Retrieved in July 2020 from https://letsreachsuccess.com/listening-to-others/.

24   Ana Holub (n.d.), Wisdomtimes. "13 Health Benefits of Forgiveness." Retrieved in July 2020 from https://www.wisdomtimes.com.

25   Nicolette, January 15, 2014. Retrieved in July 2020 from https://howdoesshe.com/why-you-should-date-your-kids-and-50-fun-date-ideas/.

26   Samantha Young, *Before Jamaica Lane*. Berkley; reprint edition, January 7, 2014.

27   Swedish blogger, October 13, 2014. Retrieved in July 2020 from https://blog.swedish.org/swedish-blog.

28   Karen Salmansohn. NotSalmon (n.d.). Retrieved in July 2020 from www.notsalmon.com.

29   Deanna Mascle, March 18, 2006. Retrieved in July 2020 from https://christian-parent.com/church-community/.

Chapter 3: Make a Difference in Your Friends and Neighbors

30   MindFuelDaily (n.d.). Retrieved in July 2020 from https://www.mindfueldaily.com.

31   Melody Pourmoradi, December 6, 2017. Retrieved in July 2020 from https://www.huffpost.com/author/mgpourmoradi-245.

32   Planned Parenthood (n.d.). Retrieved in July 2020 from https://www.plannedparenthood.org/learn/teens/bullying-safety-privacy.

33   Larry Alton, May 15, 2017. Retrieved in July 2020 from *https://www.huffpost.com/entry/a-look-at-the-incredible-benefits-of-trying-new-things_. (This page is no longer available.)*

34   Everygirl.com, September 12, 2017. Retrieved in July 2020 from https://theeverygirl.com/how-to-be-a-better-listener-with-your-friends.

35   Gary Chapman, *The Five Love Languages*. Chicago: Northfield Publishing, 1992.

36   Mark Victor Hansen (n.d.). Retrieved in June 2020 from https://www.hibiscusflorida.com/be-word/mark-victor-hansen-belief-determines-action-action-determines-results/.

Chapter 4: Make a Difference in Your Community

37   Crystal Crowder (n.d.). Retrieved in June 2020 from https://lifestyle.allwomenstalk.com/wonderful-benefits-of-writing-thank-you-notes/.

38   Diana Bruk, August 22, 2018, "8 Amazing Benefits of Having Flowers in Your Home." Retrieved in April 2022 from https://bestlifeonline.com/8-amazing-benefits-of-having-flowers-in-your-home/. Flowers and memory: A 2005 Rutgers study involved "analyzing the effect that flowers had on those aged 55 and above. The fact that the flowers boosted the moods of the senior citizens was no surprise. What was unexpected is that they seemed to have a positive impact on their episodic memory."

39   Catherine Pulsifer (n.d.), "Cheer An Inspirational Thought." Retrieved in May 2020 from https://www.wow4u.com.

40   Richard Gunderman, June 17, 2019, "The Trebek Effect: The Benefits of Well Wishes." Retrieved April 4, 2022 from https://apnews.com/article/health-cancer-the-conversation-alex-trebek-pancreatic-cancer-059852ba73c5533594a4d49f025c230c.

41   Ibid.

42   Ibid.

43   Fox news, June 22, 2017. Retrieved in April 2022 from https://www.foxnews.com/food-drink/mcdonalds-customers-in-indiana-pay-it-forward-at-drive-thru-167-times-in-a-row.

44   Diane Swanbrow, June 9, 2010, "Empathy: College students don't have as much as they used to," Michigan Today, the University of Michigan. Retrieved in April 2022 from https://michigantoday. umich.edu/2010/06/09/a7777.

45   Whitney Anthony (n.d.). Retrieved in July 2020 from https:// tinybuddha.com.

46   Jen Birch, February 18, 2015, "The Health Benefits of Reading to Children." Retrieved in July 2020 from http://blog.neurogistics. com/index.php/the-health-benefits-of-reading-to-children/.

47   Jeff Noble, March 12, 2017, "5 Reasons to Invite People to Church." Retrieved in June 2020 from https://journeyguy.com/5-reasons-to-invite-someone-to-church/.

48   Jeff Noble, September 27, 2013, "Surprises About the Unchurched." Retrieved in June 2020 from https://journeyguy.com/surprises-about-the-unchurched/.

49   Jessica Willis (n.d.), "10 Great Ways Your Family Can Clean Local Parks." Retrieved in June 2020 from *https://adventure. howstuffworks.com/10-ways-your-family-can-clean-local-parks. htm.*

50   Tracy (n.d.), "6 Inexpensive Ways to Help Your Child Love Learning." Retrieved in June 2020 from https://moneyning.com/ kids-and-money/love-learning/.

51   Georgia Douglas Johnson, "Your World," *Words with Wings: A Treasury of African-American Poetry and Art.* Harper Collins Publishers Inc., 2001. Retrieved in June 2020 from https://www. poetryfoundation.org.

52   Greater Alliance Credit Union, November 2017. Retrieved June 2020 from https://www.greateralliance.org/benefits-of-shopping-local/.

53   Our Father's House Soup Kitchen, October 31, 2019. Retrieved July 2020 from https://ofhsoupkitchen.org/why-volunteer-soupkitchen.

Chapter 5: Make a Difference in Your Country

54   Paul Hudson, July 9, 2014. Retrieved in July 2020 from https:// www.elitedaily.com/life/culture/7-reasons-reconnect.

55   Full for Life blog (n.d.), "Smile at a Stranger." Retrieved July 2020 from *https://fullforlife.com/stress-relief-and%e2%80%afgratitude%e2%80%afguide/smile-at-a-stranger/*.

56   Susie Draper (n.d.), "What Does It Mean to Be the Light?" Retrieved April 2022 from https://susiedraper.com/blog/being-the-light.

57   Patrick J. Kiger (n.d), "6 Times a Single Vote Really Did Change an Election." Retrieved in April 2022 from https://people.howstuffworks.com/can-single-vote-change-election-outcome.htm.

58   Lindsay Holmes, September 10, 2014, updated December 6, 2017, "6 Ways Being Nice to Others Is Actually Good for You." Retrieved in April 2022 from *https://www.huffpost.com/entry/facts-about-being-nice_n_5791778*.

59   Peola Hicks. Retrieved in June 2020 from *https://www.guideposts.org/stories-of-faith/discover-the-benefits-of-praying-for-others*.

60   Habitat for Humanity of Frederick County, Maryland. Retrieved in April 2022 from *https://www.frederickhabitat.org/*

61   "Habitat for Humanity's milestones in history," Retrieved in April 2021 from https://www.habitat.org/about/history/timeline.

62   HelpSaveNature.com (n.d.). Retrieved in July 2020 from https://helpsavenature.com/conserving-natural-resources.

63   Ibid.

Chapter 6: Make a Difference in Your World

64   Mayo Clinic Staff (n.d.), "Positive Thinking: Stop Negative Self-Talk to Reduce Stress." Retrieved in April 2022 from https://www.mayoclinic.org/healthy-lifestyle/stress-management/in-depth/positive-thinking/art-20043950.

65   Ibid.

66   Tania Longeau (n.d.), "Why Recycling Matters: Essential Short Term and Long Term Benefits." Retrieved in July 2020 from https://leadersinenergy.org/why-recycling-matters.

67   Worldvision.org, Hunger News Stories. Retrieved April 2022 from https://www.worldvision.org/hunger-news-stories. See also: Action Against Hunger: https://www.actionagainsthunger.org. Retrieved in June 2020.

68   Nectar Gan, January 17, 2022, "China's Birth Rate Drops for a Fifth Straight Year to Record Low," CNN Business. Retrieved April 28, 2022 from https://www.cnn.com/2022/01/17/economy/china-population-data-2021-intl-hnk/index.html.
See also: Chung Min Lee, Kathryn Botto, June 29, 2021, "Demographics and the Future of South Korea," Carnegie Endowment for International Peace. Retrieved April 28, 2022 from https://carnegieendowment.org/2021/06/29/demographics-and-future-of-south-korea-pub-84817.

69   Tamara Taraciuk Broner, March 12, 2020, "Venezuela's Health Care Crisis Now Poses A Global Threat," Retrieved April 27, 2022 from https://www.hrw.org/news/2020/03/12/venezuelas-health-care-crisis-now-poses-global-threat#:~:text=The%20country's%20health%20system%20is,steepest%20rise%20in%20malaria%20cases.

70   Eric Mertz, April 20, 2020, "China on the Verge of a Major Food Crisis – Part 1," *Nation and State*. Retrieved in April 2022 from *https://www.nationandstate.com/2022/04/20*.

71   Danuta Wasserman, Miriam Iosue, Anika Wuestefeld, Vladimir Carli, National Library of Medicine, *World Psychiatry*, September 15, 2020, "Adaptation of evidence-based suicide prevention strategies during and after the COVID-19 pandemic." Retrieved in April 2022 from *https://www.ncbi.nlm.nih.gov/pmc/articles/PMC7491639/*

72   World Vision, News & Stories / Hunger (n.d.). Retrieved in April 2022 from https://www.worldvision.org/hunger-news-stories.

73   World Health Organization (n.d.), "The Water Crisis." Retrieved in April 2022 from https://water.org/our-impact/water-crisis/.

74   Human Rights First, January 7, 2017, "Human Trafficking by the Numbers." Retrieved in April 2022 from *https://www.humanrightsfirst.org/resource/human-trafficking-numbers*.

75   Rick Warren, September 18, 2018. "10 Reasons Every Christian Should Share the Message of Jesus." Retrieved in June 2020 from https://pastors.com/10-reasons-every-christian-should-share-the-message-of-jesus/.

76   Kelly Corbett, House Beautiful, April 6, 2020. Retrieved in June 2020 from https://www.housebeautiful.com/lifestyle/a32052267/ways-to-virtually-volunteer-from-home/.

77   Jamie Booth, August, 2011, "Why Go on a Missions Trip?" Retrieved in June 2020 from *http://www.jamieebooth.com/2011/08/why-go-on-a-missions-trip/*.

78   Arianna Huffington, quote from her book *Thrive*. Retrieved in April 2022 from https://www.quotenova.net/authors/arianna-huffington/q53agd.

79   Dr. Anneke Schmidt, February 20, 2022, "7 Amazing Benefits of Keeping a Gratitude Journal." Retrieved in April 2022 from https://skillandcare.com/benefits-of-keeping-gratitude-journal.

Conclusion

80   BlissForgive, August 10, 2017, "A Story About a Man and the Boat." Retrieved in August 2020 from https://www.kindspring.org/story/view.php?sid=137702.

81   Charles Swindoll, March 17, 2020, "Risk It!" Retrieved in August 2020 from https://www.insight.org/resources/daily-devotional/individual/risk-it!1.

Want to Learn More About Donna?

To order Donna's cookbooks, *The Herbal Breads Cookbook* or *Our Favorite Recipes*;

OR

To order her culinary mixes and teas, go to Frawley's Fine Herbary website:

—— www.frawleysfineherbary.com ——

To book a speaking engagement, email Donna at donna@donnafrawley.com

Sign up for Donna's weekly newsletter to learn more about herbs, growing, and cooking, on Frawley's Fine Herbary Facebook page and click "Learn More" and get a complimentary copy of her "Dynamic Dozen."

To order additional copies of *100 Ways to Make a Difference*, go to her website: www.donnafrawley.com